The Equation of Economics

$$W = aR + (1-a)R.E$$

by

Mohammad Abu Shahadat

ISBN: 9781700335340

Contents

Unit	Contents of Unit	Page
i.	About the Author	4
ii.	Author Speech for the Reader	5
1.	Definition of Economics	7
1.1	Economics Function	8
1.2	Economics Equation	10
2.	Efficiency of a Country	12
2.1	The Rate of Efficiency	12
2.2	Indicator of a Country Grade	12
2.3	Theory of Foreign Loan and Efficiency	13
3.	The Universal Wants and The Rational Wants	14
3.1	What is Utility	18
3.2	Four Theorems for Rational Wants	19
3.3	Difference between Wants and Needs	24
3.4	The Stage of Wants and Needs	26
3.5	Expansion of Wants of an Individual	28
4.	Economic Resources	35
4.1	Human Resources	36
4.2	Natural Resources	37
4.3	Depreciation	43
4.4	Economic Efficiency	46
5.	First Atom of the Universe	47
5.1.	Center Point Theory	49
5.2.	Calculation of Radius and Area of the Universe	54
6.	Location of Angels, Aliens and Animals	64
6.1.	Angels	64
6.2.	Aliens	65
6.3.	Animals	70
6.4.	Theory of Travelling Time in the Universe	70
7.	Theory of the Global Warming	73
7.1.	Fundamental Concept of Global Warming	74

	Model	
7.2.	Global Warming Micro Model	75
7.3.	Global Warming Macro Model	83
7.4.	Some Function for Global Warming	87
7.5.	Who are responsible for Global Warming	90
7.6.	How to Reduce the Global Warming	91
7.7.	Turning the Present World into the Green World	95

To write Unit 4 I have taken help from the various honorable writers and various web sides. I am grateful to them.

About The Author

Mohammad Abu Shahadat

Founder & Headteacher, Notre Damian School
Student, Welfare Economic System since 2013
BSS (Hon's), MSS in (Economics), Jagannath University
Studied from 2002 to 2004 at Notre Dame College,
from 1997 to 2002 at Delpara High School and
from 1992 to 1996 at MDC Model Institute
Born on 14 January 1987, Dhaka, Bangladesh

www.amazon.com/Mohammad-Abu-Shahadat/e/B07WC912RD

Contact: www.facebook.com/MAbuShahadat
Email: mabu.shahadat@gmail.com
Cell Phone: +8801682744844

The Author's Speech for The Readers

I founded Welfare Economic System and Development in 2013. Since then to develop the welfare economic system I individually have been working and researching. Without the mystery of the universe and global warming solution I cannot complete the Welfarism. Moreover, as no scientist or researcher has not still discovered the location of alien, the mystery of graviton particles, center of the universe and first atom, I have written these researchful topics with my little knowledge.

Almost all Economists have discussed with literature that wants are unlimited but resources are limited . I have tried to make Economics equation and discuss mathematically various topics on Economics. To write various topics I have to take help from different writers' articles and web sides. I am grateful to them.

Dear readers and followers, I am none without you. I always try to write different topics. So if you find any mistake please inform me by email.

My family is trying to educate our students with qualified teachers. Students of our school come from various economic groups but they get equal opportunities to learn. We hope, we will create future Newton, Einstein, Socrates, Pythagoras and so on. Thanks for reading this section.

As an individual I can help few numbers of children and adolescences but with the help of sympathetic big hearted people like you I can help a large number of children and adolescences of my locality.

Daily we are spending lots of money for nothing or some random pointless reason but from your daily that money a little amount ($ 1 to $ 5 or more according to your capacity) can ensure education for most of our students who do not get enough food for their meals and quality education . A little donation from you can make our students happy and can receive education up to SSC (Secondary School Certificate) level which is equivalent O level education .

We are helping 76 students this year (2019) and that's just not enough. With your help we can help more students than ever. EVERY DOLLAR HELPS so give whatever feels comfortable to you. All of the money raised will spend directly for the students' educational expenses. Such as:

- One meal per day for students (6 days per week)
- Two set school uniform for the students per year.
- Books and supplies
- Salaries for the teachers
- Classwise monthly stipend for the brilliant students

If any one wishes to donate any amount to run our school , I will leave my bank account details below.

FSIB
Branch: Ranavola
Account Name : Mohammad Abu Shahadat
Account No. 022812200003539
Or , Please send the amount by Bkash - +880682744844

Thank you for all your support.

Mohammad Abu Shahadat

16 October 2019

Dhaka, Bangladesh

Definition of Economics

I think Economics is a branch of science and all branches of science work for Economics. It is the study of how economic agents collectively satisfy needs of a society or country and research for turning desires into needs. We know that wants are unlimited. But I think rational wants are limited. Wants is the summation of needs and desires.

Economic agents are consumers, producers, sleeping partners of business organizations, government, international traders and welfare organizations. All are consumers but all consumers are not producers or sleeping partners of business.

Our resources are limited but efficiency (knowledge and technology) is less than infinity. The more an individual develops his / her efficiency the more he / she can satisfy his / her wants. The more a country develops its human resource the more it can fulfil the wants of its population and other countries for welfare.

Through research the desires of today will turn into the needs of tomorrow. So in short time wants cannot be measured by money and seem to be unlimited. But in long time wants can be measured by money. Then rational wants will be limited.

For an example, before 1969 men had desire to go to the moon. Men developed their efficiency by acquiring knowledge and researching various empirical test. Finally they invented rocket and space craft to go to the moon. After 1969 going to the moon is needs of the rich visitors to spend various vacations. The expenditure of visiting the moon can be measured by money and it is very expensive. Perhaps one day the cost of visiting the moon will be as cheap as the mobile phone because of the next generation's research and experiments or high efficiency of mankind. Another example is the invention of the plane. Once upon a time men had a desire to fly in the sky like birds. Man thought "If I had the wings of a bird!" It was then man's desire. Some men tried again and again how to fly in the sky. After developing efficiency on how to fly in the sky the Wright brothers turned desires into needs in 1904 by inventing fly machine.

In brief, Economics is a study of how an individual or a country satisfies rational wants with resources and efficiency.

Economics Function

Function means the dependent variable is determined by the independent variable or variables.

A function is a mathematical relationship in which the values of a single dependent variable are determined by the values of one or more independent variables.

Independent variables are those which do not depend on other variables. Dependent variable is that is changed by the independent variables. The change is caused by the independent variable or variables. For example, an individual's income is the independent variable and the consumption is the dependent variable.

In Economics, rational wants (W) is a dependent variable. Resources (R) and the efficiency (E) are two independent variables.

Economics function is a relationship in which the value of rational want is determined by the values of resources and the efficiency.

Functions with a single independent variable are called univariate functions. There is a one to one correspondence. Functions with more than one independent variable are called multivariate functions. Economics function is a multivariate function.

We say W is a function of R and E. This means W depends on or is determined by R and E

Mathematically we write, $W = f(R, E)$

It means that mathematically W depends on R and E. If we know the value of R and E, then we can find the value of W. In pronunciation we say "W is function of R and E."

Therefore, the economics function is, $W = f(R, E)$

Where,

W = Rational Wants

R = Limited Resources

E = Efficiency

f = sign of function

W is a dependent variable and R and E are the two independent variables.

Economics Equation

Rational wants is the summation of Needs and Desires.

$W = N + D$

Where, W = Rational Wants

N = Needs

D = Desires

$N = f(R) = aR$ --------- (i)

To satisfy needs we require a part of resources.

$a = \Delta N / \Delta R$ = the marginal propensity to utilize Resources

$D = f(E) = (1-a)R.E$ -------------- (ii)

To satisfy desires we require efficiency and rest of the resources

Adding (i) and (ii) we get,

$$N + D = aR + (1-a)R.E$$

$\Rightarrow W = aR + (1-a)R.E$ [since, $W = N + D$]

Therefore,

the Equation of the Economics is, $W = aR + (1-a)R.E$

where $0 \leq E < \infty$ and $0 \leq a \leq 1$,

W represents rational wants which is less than the Universal Wants (W_U).

It means $W < W_U$

The more the value of E increases the more the probable value of W increases.

$a = \Delta W / \Delta R$

$a = 1$, It means that a country utilizes its resources for needs. This country is called the needy country and its $(1-a) RE = 0$. It has no any desires. So the efficiency of this country has no usefulness.

$a = 0$, it means the country has no need. It utilizes its all resources for turning desires into needs.

The more the value of a increases, the more the country's economy depends on the developed or developing countries to utilize the natural resources by hiring the efficiency and trying to develop the efficiency.

$E > 0$ means developing efficiency

$E = 0$ means no efficiency

in micro sense, the efficiency of the rich persons like Bill Gates is infinite and his $E < \infty$. On the other hand, a beggar has no efficiency and his $E = 0$. In macro sense, the efficiency of the developed and developing countries is $E < \infty$

GNI = Gross National Income

NNI = Net National Income

NNI is less than GNI
That is, NNI < GNI

Efficiency of a Country

Efficiency of a country is the quotient of NNI and population.
E = NNI / Population

Where, E = Efficiency
NNI = GNI – Depreciation – foreign loan
Population = Total population of a country

Rate of Efficiency
= {(GNI – Depreciation – foreign loan) / GNI} x 100
= (NNI / GNI) x 100

Indicator of a country grade (θ)

Θ = (NNI / GNI) x 90^0
we can determine the nature of the financial condition of a country by the indicator of the country grade. The value of θ indicates the nature of a country. If the county has negative value of Theta (θ < 0) it means the country has no efficiency and dependent on other countries. This type of country is called the extreme poor country. If 0 < θ < 3°, then the country is called poor country. If 3° < θ < 10° then the country is called the least developing country . If 10° < θ < 20° then the country is called the developing country. If 20° < θ < 30° then the country is called the super developing country. If 30° < θ < 45° then the country is called the lowest developed country. If 45° < θ < 50° then the country is called the optimum developed

country. If 50° < θ < 60° then the country is called the C grade developed country. If 60° < θ < 70° then the country is called the B grade developed country. If 70° < θ < 80° then the country is called the A grade developed country. If 80° < θ < 90° then the country is called the A+ grade developed country. If 90° < θ < 180° then the country is called the excellent developed country.

Theory of Efficiency and Foreign Loan

The more the efficiency increases, the more foreign loan will decrease.
There is a negative relationship between efficiency and foreign loan.
Foreign loan (L) depends on Efficiency (E).
The function is, $L = f(E) = bE$ Where, $-1 \leq b \leq 0$
$b = \Delta L / \Delta E = (L_f - L_o) / (E_f - E_0)$
where,
L_f = the final amount of foreign loan
L_o = the initial amount of foreign loan
E_f = the final amount of efficiency
E_0 = the initial amount of efficiency
$b = 0$, it means a country need not loan. The country is self-dependent for construction of its highway, bridges, buildings, flyovers etc.
$b = -1$, it means a country need foreign loan to run economic activities

The Universal Wants and the Rational Wants

In dream, we get what we want without any cost. All wants can be fulfilled there. So in dream or heaven there is no economics because there price is equal to zero and unlimited demand is less than unlimited supply like we find in the sea water, sunlight, air etc. But in the real world the more we get the more we want in the context of time interval with the passage of the advancing modern world. We find unlimited wants are more than limited resources and efficiency. If the rational or irrational wants under discussion are included in a particular want, that particular want is called the Universal Want (W_U). It is infinite. It is like an infinite series. Such as $W_U = w_1 + w_2 + w_3 + w_4 + \ldots\ldots + w_n + \ldots\ldots$. Our wants are unlimited like the sky. We cannot reach the last point of the sky from the world. But we can reach the sum of partial points of the sky like the moon, the mars or other planets with the help of technology which is considered to me the efficiency. Like the sum of partial points of the sky we can satisfy our wants with our limited resources and efficiency. Where we would like to reach to satisfy our wants is the sum of partial points of the Universal Wants. The sum of partial points of the Universal wants is considered as Rational Wants. Deficit budget of a country is also the sum of partial points of wants. By infinite series we can calculate the sum of the Rational Wants.

The n th term of an arithmetic series $= f + (n-1)d$

the sum of the first n th term of the series = $(n/2)\{2f + (n-1)d\}$

where, f = the first term,

d = common difference = the 2nd term – the 1st term

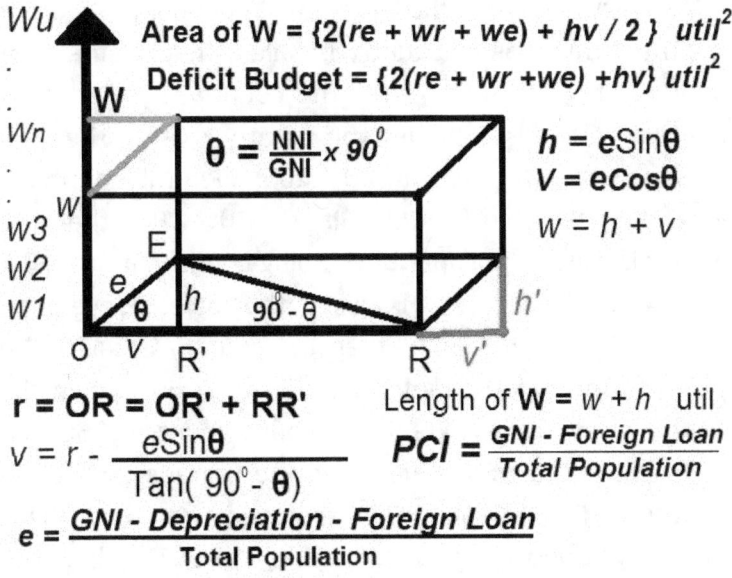

Figure 1

the sum of w and h of a solid rectangular is considered as the length of rational wants of a country. The length (r), the breadth (e) and the height (w) are the element of a solid rectangular. The value of the limited Resource (R) is known to an individual or a firm or a country. But the values of e, w, v, h are unknown. With the help of my design any one can easily find out the other values. An individual or business firm or a country can calculate how much efficiency needs to reach the desire point of wants with the limited resources. We can calculate the rational wants where we would like to reach or satisfy wants. Moreover, we can determine the nature of the financial condition of a country by the indicator of the country grade. The value of θ indicates the nature of a country. If the county has negative value of Theta ($\theta < 0$) it means the country has no efficiency and dependent on other countries. This type of country is called the extreme poor country. If $0 < \theta < 3°$, then the country is called poor country. If $3° < \theta < 10°$ then the country is called the least developing country. If $10° < \theta < 20°$ then the country is called the developing country. If $20° < \theta < 30°$ then the country is called the super developing country. If $30° < \theta < 45°$ then the country is called the lowest developed country. If $45° < \theta < 50°$ then the country is called the optimum developed country. If $50° < \theta < 60°$ then the country is called the C grade developed country. If $60° < \theta < 70°$ then the country is called the B grade developed country. If $70° < \theta < 80°$ then the country is called the A grade developed country. If $80° < \theta < 90°$ then the country is called the A+ grade developed country. If $90° < \theta < 180°$ then the country is called the excellent developed country.

Where, GNI means Gross National Income

GNI = GDP + money flowing from foreign countries − money flowing to foreign countries

GDP means Gross Domestic Products

GDP is a monetary measure of the market value of all the final goods and services produced in a specific time period.

Foreign loan to a country made by foreign governments or financial organization are called foreign loans.

PCI means per capita income.

PCI = (GNI − Foreign Loan) / Total Population

The area of the rational wants = $\{2\,(re + wr + ew) + hv/2\}$ util^2

The length of Rational wants = $(w + h)$ Util

$$= h + v + h \quad util$$

$$= 2h + v \quad util$$

$$= 2 \cdot e\sin\Theta + \{r - e\sin\Theta / \tan(90^0 - \Theta)\}$$

Util is the unit of utility.

Deficit budget = $\{2\,(re + wr + ew) + hv\}$ util^2

A budget deficit occurs when an individual, business or government budgets more spending than there is revenue available to pay for the spending, over a specific period of time. Loan is the aggregate value of deficits accumulated over time. In the formula of the deficit budget, to satisfy $hv/2$ the country or organization or individual should take loan. The amount of loan will be **v′**.

What is utility ?

Economic activities are occurred for the utility. Producers create the utility of goods and services. They also import the utility of goods and services. Money is used for the medium of exchange. Consumers satisfy the utility of goods and services. Producers export the utility of commodities. The Government takes taxes from consumers and producers and develop the environment of infrastructure to create investment for the sake of helping producers create the utility of goods and services.

Utility is the power of goods or services to satisfy consumers wants. The unit of it is util. Util can be measured by money.

1 util = the quantity of purchased goods and services / amount of money for buying that goods and services

1 util of luxury goods or services > 1 util of daily necessities > 1 gifen goods

1 mimi util = 0.001 util

1 centi util = 0.01 util

1 deci util = 0.1 util

1 deca util = 10 util

1 Hecto util = 100 util

1 kiloutil = 1000 util

1 Mega util = 1000000 util

1 Giga Util = 1000000000 util

1 Tera util = 10^{12} util

1 Peta util = 10^{15} util

1 Exa util = 10^{18} util

The producer of goods and services create utility and consumer satisfy their utility of goods and services by money.

Four Theorems for Rational Wants

The angular triangle of Resources indicates to satisfy this wants the country should wait for future or take loan. To take loan is not good.

Theorem 1. The area of the rational wants is more than the area of a solid rectangular.

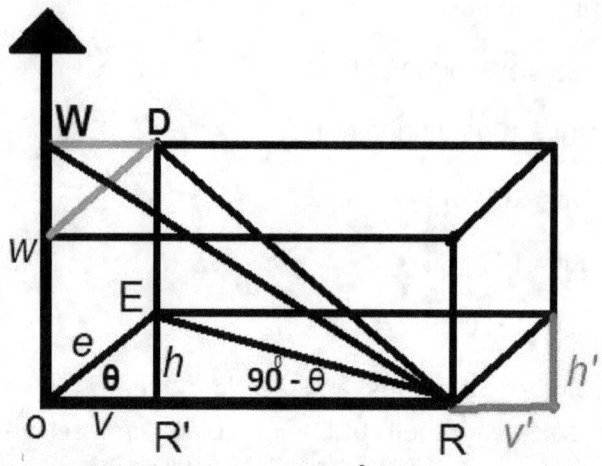

here, $r = OR$, $OE = e$, $w = h + v$

The area of a solid rectangular = $2(re + wr + ew)$

The area of the rational wants = $2(re + wr + ew) + hv/2$

Figure 2 for Theorem 1

We know, The area of a solid rectangular = $2(re + wr + ew)$

The area of the rational wants = $2(re + wr + ew) + hv/2$

Difference = $2(re + wr + ew) + hv/2 - 2(re + wr + ew) = hv/2$

So, the area of rational wants > the area of a solid rectangular

Theorem 2. The area of angular triangle of rational wants creates opposite side the same area of angular triangle unfulfilled wants. If we try to satisfy the unfulfilled wants the country will have to borrow or wait for the future efficiency.

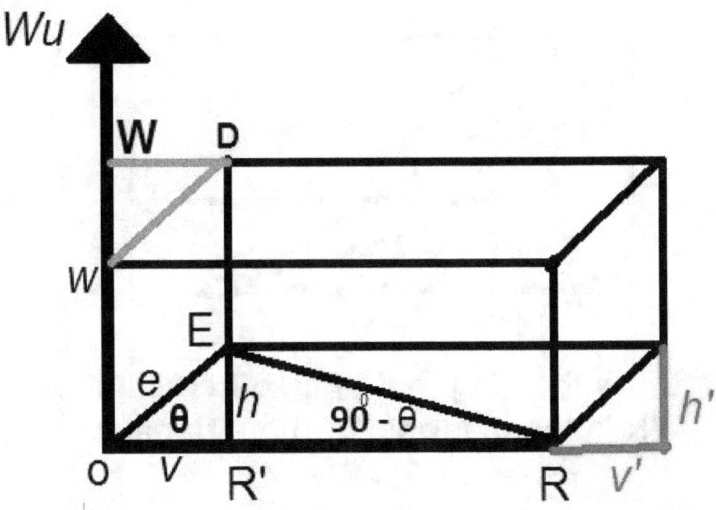

In figure, Δ WDw = Δ Rv'h'.   OR = Limited Resources

If we would like to satisfy the area of Δ Rv'h' we have to increase resources upto v'. How can we increase resources the amount Rv'? We have to borrow or wait for the future efficiency. When our efficiency increases, we will fulfil the unfulfilled wants.

Theorem 3. The diagonal of the rational want is greater than the diagonal of a solid rectangular.

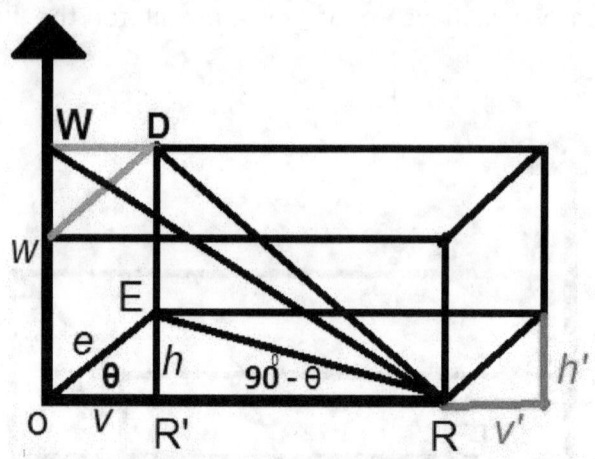

DR is the diagonal of a solid rectangular
WR is the diagonal of the rational wants
here, WR > DR

Theorem 4. The deficit budget is greater than the area of rational wants.

The area of the rational wants = $\{2(re + wr + ew) + hv/2\}$ util^2

Deficit budget = $\{2(re + wr + ew) + hv\}$ util^2

Since, hv is greater than $hv/2$

Therefore,

$\{2(re + wr + ew) + hv\} > \{2(re + wr + ew) + hv/2\}$

So, Deficit budget > the area of the rational wants

In fine, our resources are limited but efficiency (knowledge and technology) is less than infinity. The more an individual develops his or her efficiency the more he or she can satisfy his or her wants. The more a country develops its human resource the more it can fulfil the wants of its population and other countries for welfare.

The Rational Wants of an individual or a society or country is definite and it has a definite expansion. The budget of a country depends on the rational wants. $W_U = \infty$ and $W_R < W_U$. Rational Wants of an individual depends on marginal income (minimum wage) which is declared by the wage board of the country where he or she lives and his or her efficiency. The government of a country declared minimum wage per month or per year for its employment. Annually or in the interval of time the minimum wage is changeable due to the standard of living. But in the current year the minimum wage is constant. The efficiency is always changeable because of gathering experience and acquiring knowledge. The efficiency is increasing with the passage of time. So, in micro sense, the rational wants of an individual depends on two variables. They are his minimum wage and the efficiency. In macro sense, The Rational Wants of a country depends on MITP and human resources. MITP denotes the marginal income of total population. To reach the apex of the rational wants economic agents collectively have been working since the dawn of civilization. For this many socio-economic problems happen and these problems are tried to solve by economic agents. In an economy consumers or individuals or households, producers or firms or business organizations, the sleeping partners of business, government, international traders and welfare organization etc. are called economic agents.

Difference between Wants and Needs

Needs are an element of wants. Wants have two elements. They are needs and desires. So the equation of wants is $W = N + D$ where W denotes wants, N denotes needs and D denotes desires. Resources is required to satisfy needs but efficiency is required for satisfying desires. The function of needs is, $N = f(R)$ and the function of desires is $D = f(E)$ where R implies resources and E implies efficiency. There are positive relationship between needs (N) and resources (R). The more resources increase the more needs will satisfy. Desires (D) and efficiency (E) also have positive relationship. The more efficiency develops the more desires will fulfil. So the equation of wants is $W = N + D = f(R) + f(E)$

All needs are wants but all wants are not needs. Needs can be measured by money and needs has a definite value. But money cannot measure desires. To measure desire we require the formula of probability. We will get a probable value of desires. Through research the desires of today will turn into the needs of tomorrow.

For an example, before 1969 men had desire to go to the moon. Men developed their efficiency by acquiring knowledge and researching various empirical test. Finally they invented rocket and space craft to go to the moon. After 1969 going to the moon is needs of the rich visitors to spend various vacations. The expenditure of visiting the moon can be measured by money and it is very expensive. Perhaps one day the cost of visiting the moon will be as cheap as the mobile phone because of the next generation's research and experiments or high efficiency of mankind. Another example is the invention of the plane. Once upon a time men had a desire to fly in the sky like birds. Man thought "If I had the wings of a bird!" It was then man's desire. Some men tried again and again how to fly in the sky. After developing efficiency on how to fly in the sky the Wright brothers turned desires into needs in 1904 by inventing fly machine. An interesting example of turning desire into needs. After completing MSS in Economics in 2009. I had a desire to introduce a new economic system for peace. Since then I have been writing and opened a page on facebook named Welfare Economic System and Development (WESD) and trying to acquire knowledge about various economic systems like capitalism, socialism, Islamic economy and mixed economy. I've found and still find more economic oppressions in the capitalistic economy than most other economic systems. I am thinking and writing how to minimize or eradicate economic oppressions from society. Instead of searching jobs I am thinking of how to introduce welfare economic system. How mad I am! I worked as a teacher in some schools for living. However, I have found Notre Damian School in 2018 to educate children and adolescences especially poor students for welfare. Finally I have written this book which you (dear reader) are reading now. Thus I have turn my desire into needs for others.

Our wants are unlimited like the sky. We cannot reach the last point of the sky from the world. But we can reach the sum of partial points of the sky like the moon, the mars or other planets with the help of technology which is considered to me the efficiency. Like the sum of partial points of the sky we can satisfy our wants with our limited resources and efficiency. Where we would like to reach to satisfy our wants is the sum of partial points of the Universal Wants. The sum of partial points of the Universal wants is considered as Rational Wants. Deficit budget of a country is also the sum of partial points of wants. By infinite series we can calculate the sum of the Rational Wants and by the binomial expansion we can calculate the expansion of the Rational Wants .

The Stage of needs and wants

Time is continuous. Needs are the minimum necessary goods and services required for human existence. Such as food, clothes, shelter, education and health. On the other hand, Wants are goods and services that are not compulsory for life. Such as the quality of food, quality of clothes, quality of shelter, quality of education , quality of health, quality of entertainment and quality of transportation. Wants depend on individuals' efficiency. On the basis of efficiency individuals select an item among homogenous items but different qualities. A man's first need is food for survival. So the first stage of needs depends on food. The function of 1st need is N1 = f (F) Where, N1 = need and F = food

In this stage individual doesn't choose the quality of food. Rather he is happy to satisfy his demand. Satisfying 1st stage of needs he wants to fulfil next needs.

The function of 2nd stage of needs is N2 = f(F, C) where, N2 = Needs, F = Food and C = Clothes. After fulfilling the 2nd stage of needs he wishes to reach the 3rd stage of needs. The function of the 3rd stage of needs is N3 = f(F,C,S) where, S= shelter

After reaching the 3rd stage of needs he desires to satisfy the 4th stage of needs and the function of the 4th stage of needs is N4 =f(F,C,S,E) where, E = Education.

After reaching the 4th stage he likes to satisfy the last basic need which is health. The function of the 5th stage is N5 = f(F,C,S,E,H) where, H = Health. As soon as he satisfies the minimum necessary needs, He will feel lack of better standard of living. Since then wants run after him. He searches the best quality of products with the limitation of his resources based on efficiency. The group of wants function of him is W = f(Fq , Cq ,Sq, Eq, Hq, Rq,Tq, P, S,Tx ,Wlfr) where q = quality, R = Recreation (Entertainment) , T = Transportation . P = Power and fuel , S = Savings, Tx = Tax and Wlfr = Welfare for the poor

Space travelling, visiting places, watching movies and games etc are element of entertainment. Grants and monetary help are elements of welfare.

Quality of economic goods and services depends on efficiency. Efficiency depends on productivity. The mathematical term of quality of economic products is Qep = f (E) and E = f(pt) where Qep = The quality of economic products, E = efficiency and pt = Productivity.

Expansion of Wants of an Individual

Group of wants = Food + Clothes + Shelter + Education + Health + Transportation + Power and fuel + Entertainment + Savings + Welfare + ...

Wants of an individual or household depends on total income(TI). TI depends on both marginal wage (mw) and efficiency (E). The marginal wage is estimated by wage board of the country where the individual lives.

The equation of TI is, TI = mw + E

mw has a definite numerical value but E has either numerical value or probable value.

He applies TI to satisfy his wants. But his wants is less than Universal Want. So with his total income he can fulfil his want group. His wants group's expansion is equals to $(mw + E)^n$ where, n = the number of element of wants group.

Normally there are ten elements in a group of wants. They are food, clothes, shelter, education, health, transportation, power and fuel, entertainment, savings and welfare. Here, the element number of wants is 10 (ten). So the wants expansion of a family or an individual is (Total income)^n = (Total income)^{10}

Therefore, EW = $(w + e)^{10}$ where, EW = expansion wants

According to the Binomial Expansion

$(w + e)^{10} = \sum_{k=0}^{10} \binom{10}{k} w^k e^{10-k}$ = T1 + T2 + T3 + T4 + T5 + T6 + T7 + T8 + T9 + T10 + T11

Here, n = 10

n = 10,9,8,7,6,5,4,3,2,1,0

k = 0,1,2,3,4,5,6,7,8,9,10

If n = k, then n − k = 0

$\binom{n}{n} = 1$

$\binom{n}{0} = 1$

$w^0 = 1$

The number of terms (T) = n + 1

T1 = $\binom{10}{0} w^{10} e^{10-10} = 1 \cdot w^{10} e^0 = w^{10} \cdot 1 = w^{10}$

T2 = $\binom{10}{1} w^{10-1} e^{10-9} = \binom{10}{1} w^9 e^1 = \binom{10}{1} w^9 e$

T3 = $\binom{10}{2} w^{10-2} e^{10-8} = \binom{10}{2} w^8 e^2$

$$T4 = \binom{10}{3}w^{10-3}e^{10-7} = \binom{10}{3}w^7e^3$$

$$T5 = \binom{10}{4}w^{10-4}e^{10-6} = \binom{10}{4}w^6e^4$$

$$T6 = \binom{10}{5}w^{10-5}e^{10-5} = \binom{10}{5}w^5e^5$$

$$T7 = \binom{10}{6}w^{10-6}e^{10-4} = \binom{10}{6}w^4e^6$$

$$T8 = \binom{10}{7}w^{10-7}e^{10-3} = \binom{10}{7}w^3e^7$$

$$T9 = \binom{10}{8}w^{10-8}e^{10-2} = \binom{10}{8}w^2e^8$$

$$T10 = \binom{10}{9}w^{10-9}e^{10-1} = \binom{10}{9}w^1e^9$$

$$T11 = \binom{10}{10}w^{10-10}e^{10-0} = \binom{10}{10}w^0e^{10} = 1.1.\, e^{10} = e^{10}$$

EW = T1 + T2 + T3 + T4 + T5 + T6 + T7 + T8 + T9 + T10 + T11

$$\Rightarrow EW = w^{10} + \binom{10}{1}w^9e + \binom{10}{2}w^8e^2 + \binom{10}{3}w^7e^3 +$$
$$\binom{10}{4}w^6e^4 + \binom{10}{5}w^5e^5 + \binom{10}{6}w^4e^6 + \binom{10}{7}w^3e^7$$
$$+ \binom{10}{8}w^2e^8 + \binom{10}{9}we^9 + e^{10}$$

$\Rightarrow EW = w^{10} + 10w^9 e + \dfrac{10.9}{1.2} w^8 e^2 + \dfrac{10.9.8}{1.2.3} w^7 e^3 + \dfrac{10.9.8.7}{1.2.3.4} w^6 e^4 + \dfrac{10.9.8.7.6}{1.2.3.4.5} w^5 e^5 + \dfrac{10.9.8.7.6.5}{1.2.3.4.5.6} w^4 e^6 + \dfrac{10.9.8.7.6.5.4}{1.2.3.4.5.6.7} w^3 e^7 + \dfrac{10.9.8.7.6.5.4.3}{1.2.3.4.5.6.7.8} w^2 e^8 + \dfrac{10.9.8.7.6.5.4.3.2}{1.2.3.4.5.6.7.8.9} w e^9 + e^{10}$

$\Rightarrow EW = w^{10} + 10 w^9 e + 45 w^8 e^2 + 120 w^7 e^3 + 210 w^6 e^4 + 252 w^5 e^5 + 210 w^4 e^6 + 120 w^3 e^7 + 45 w^2 e^8 + 10 w e^9 + e^{10}$

Since, w = minimum wage per hour which is declared by the authority of the country base year so w is a constant value. In Bangladesh the minimum wage in 2019 is Tk. 8250 per month.

If the value of efficiency increases the quantity of wants expansion will increase. The relationship between wants expansion and efficiency is positive. The marginal wage is constant value which is estimated by the declaration of the authority of a country. n goes from n to o and k goes from o to n.

To solve this equation we have to learn about the factorial number and some exponent formula.

n! (factorial n) = n(n-1) (n-2) (n-3) (n-4) ………. 4.3.2.1

Now we can understand this equation very easy.

1! = 1

2! = 2.1 = 2

3! = 3.2.1 = 6

4! = 4.3.2.1 = 24

5! = 5.4.3.2.1 = 120

6! = 6.5.4.3.2.1 = 720

7! = 7.6.5.4.3.2.1 = 5040

8! = 8.7.6.5.4.3.2.1 = 40320

9! = 9.8.7.6.5.4.3.2.1 = 362880

10! = 10.9.8.7.6.5.4.3.2.1 = 3628800

10! = 10.9.8.7.6.5.4.3.2.1 = 3628800

9! = 9.8.7.6.5.4.3.2.1 = 362880

8! = 8.7.6.5.4.3.2.1 = 40320

7! = 7.6.5.4.3.2.1 = 5040

6! = 6.5.4.3.2.1 = 720

5! = 5.4.3.2.1 = 120

4! = 4.3.2.1 = 24

3! = 3.2.1 = 6

2! = 2.1 = 2

1! = 1

The Individual requires to choose which the most important want among his desiring wants is. Then he tries to fulfil the most important want by limited resources and efficiency. If efficiency develops the most important want (MIW) will be satisfied with minimum resource within minimum times. Consequently the rest of the resources will save. Then he tries to fulfil his second important want with efficiency and saving resources.

Needs are limited but Wants are unlimited. Resources are limited but efficiency is unlimited. Only limited resources require to satisfy needs but both limited resources and efficiency require to fulfil wants.

Efficiency is unlimited because to develop efficiency it requires to acquire knowledge which is unlimited. An individual has to go to his working place by bus. He can satisfy this needs by buying a ticket with his enough money to travel by bus to go to his destination. But if he likes to go to the moon, he will require both enough money to go to the moon and efficiency to travel by space craft.

The function of needs is $N = f(R)$ and the function of wants is $W = f(R, E)$

Then we can say that the range of Needs or Resources is $0 < N = R < \infty$ and the equation of Unlimited wants and Efficiency is $W = E = \infty$ (infinity)

A society faces a problem to satisfy its most important want with limited resources and efficiency. The problem :

MIW > R where MIW= the most important want, R = Limited Resources.

To solve the problem the society needs efficiency (E) where E is greater than zero.

E > 0. The more the value of efficiency(E) increases the less the quantity of resources applies and the more the quantity of resources will save. Finally if the society gets aR > MIW, it will try to fulfil its next important want. But if the society gets aR = MIW, it will cannot expect to fulfil its next important want. If it desires to satisfy its next important want, it will borrow loans from other society. This is not good for the society. To borrow loans means depending on others.

The quantity of W is equals to the amount of budget of a country.

UW = ∞

W < UW

The quantity of W depends on the value of n. The more the value of n increases the more the quantity of W will increase.

N is a set of natural number. N = { 1,2,3,4,5,6……. } and n is an element of N

The quantity of W = arithmetic series or geometric series

In arithmetic series, The quantity of W = $n/2\{ 2f + (n-1)d \}$

Here, f = 1ˢᵗ term of the series, d= common difference = 2ⁿᵈ term − 1ˢᵗ term

From this infinite series a society has to select a level for *W* according to its resource and efficiency. If it has no enough resources and efficiency (human resources) to fulfil the level of want. It has to develop its human resources. One day it will reach this want level.

Resources are limited. Due to war, natural disasters and G7-made global warming resources are declining slowly. G7 means the group of seven capitalist countries. They are United States the extreme capitalist, The United Kingdom, Canada, France, Italy, Germany and Japan. I think these countries are the followers of the Fed, the central bank of the United States. Due to human resources the efficiency is increasing day by day. As a result a country can manage to increase its resources by exporting goods and services and to take necessary steps to minimize loss of resources against natural disasters such as earthquakes, cyclones etc. and the capitalist-made war and economic oppressions. If there are no resources, an economy cannot be sustained.

Economic Resources

There are four types of factors of production. They are land, labor, capital, and entrepreneurship. The first factor of production is land, but this includes any natural resource used to produce goods and services. Labor and entrepreneurship are called human resource. Capital is related with all man-made resources such as financial resources and machineries. When we combine all of factors, we get production.

What are the characteristics of resources?
There are certain basic characteristics of resources.
1. Resources are limited both qualitatively and quantitatively
2. Resources are Useful
3. Resources are interrelated and interdependent
4. Resources have alternative uses
5. One resource may be substituted for another

Human Resources
Labor is one of the common factors of production. Without mental and physical labor nothing can be produced according to Economics. There are two kinds of labor. They are production labor and service labor. An example of production labor is any factory worker. Service labor includes people involved in providing a service, such as doctors, teachers, bankers, lawyers, accountants, sales people, mechanics, and plumbers.

The another name of entrepreneurship is management. As organizations became more complex with the onset of the Industrial Revolution, employees were required to oversee and manage the masses of workers engaged in the production process. Management is a resource that is used to facilitate efficient and effective production or operations of a business so that it can accomplish its goals. Rather than being directly involved in production or services, managers coordinate, monitor and direct employees engaged in the production or service.

Nonhuman Resources
Land and capital are called nonhuman resources. Land is all real estate and all natural resources on or in it, such as trees, minerals, elements, metals, gems, natural gas, thermal heat, oil, coal, water, and crops. Capital is related with all man-made resources such as financial resources and machineries.

Natural Resources

Natural resources are elements that exist in the world without the participation of humans. These natural resources are diverse ranging from renewable resources to non-renewable resources, living to non-living resources, tangible to intangible resources. Natural resources are important to the existence of humans and all other living beings. All the goods in the world use natural resources as their basic element, which may be water, air, natural chemicals or energy. The high demand for natural resources around the world has led to their rapid reduction. As a result, most countries are pushing for proper supervision and bearable use of natural resources.

Types Of Natural Resources
Natural resources could be classified into different categories such as renewable and non-renewable resources, biotic and abiotic resources, and stock resources.

Renewable Natural Resources
Renewable resources denote resources that can naturally regenerate after use. They include resources such as wind,

water, natural vegetation, solar energy, and animals. These resources exist in nature in abundance. There is little concern about depleting renewable resources because their rate of production exceeds the rate of human consumption. Conservationists throughout the world advocate for the use of renewable resources because they are readily available and less costly to the environment.

Non-renewable Natural Resources
Non-renewable resources are components that take too long to refill after use or exist in limited quantities. Non-renewable resources include products such as crude oil, precious metals, minerals, and rocks. Some endangered animals are also classified as non-renewable resources because their mortality rate is much higher than their reproduction rate. These non-renewable resources need to be protected and to be used responsibly to stop their depletion.

Biotic Natural Resources
Biotic natural resources refer to living resources that exist naturally in the environment. Such resources include forests, wildlife, and fossil fuels, which are all listed as biotic natural resources.

Non-biotic Natural Resources
Non-biotic natural resources are natural products in the surroundings that are non-living. These resources include water, rocks, metals, and minerals among many others.

Stock Natural Resources
The world has numerous resources some of which are yet to be exploited. Humans lack the skills and technology to extract and use some of the naturally occurring resources like rare gases and some radioactive materials. As a result,

these resources are classified as stock resources to be utilized in the future.

Threats To Natural Resources

Most natural resources exist in limited quantities. Unfortunately, various factors have led to the exploitation of these resources. Some of the components are at the risk of depletion. Environmental pollution, high population, uncontrolled development, climate change, and modern lifestyles are some of the threats to natural resources.

Environmental Pollution

Environmental pollution has been the leading cause of natural resources degradation and depletion. Environmental pollution is mainly caused by industries that produce and use chemicals and plastics in their operations. These chemicals sip into the soil and water systems and alter the composition of the resources. The increased use of harsh chemicals and plastics in the environment has led to destruction of aquatic life.

High Population Levels

The world's human population has significantly increased in the past five decades. As the number of people rises, so does the demand for natural resources. People have over-exploited resources such as water, agricultural land, minerals and wildlife leading to depletion of most natural resources in some parts of the world. Countries that have uncontrolled population increase often put pressure on the limited natural resources leading to environmental degradation.

Unsustainable Development

Most countries have experienced rapid development with the creation of new industries and infrastructure. These development projects require lots of resources such as land, energy, water and human resource. In some cases, development has encroached on forests or protected land and led to the destruction of significant vegetation and wildlife. It is, therefore, necessary to control the development to prevent overutilization of limited and endangered resources.

Climate Change
Climate change is a reality in the current world. The effects of climate change have been excessive flooding, extreme weather conditions, earthquakes, and other calamities. These changes have threatened the way of life of numerous species leading to the extinction of some. Forest fires caused by climate change have also resulted in the destruction of forests which are valuable natural resources.

Modern Lifestyles
The modern society is the most advanced society in human history. Due to the advanced way of life, more resources are needed to meet the many demands humans have. For instance, people consume so much energy through vehicles on the roads, electronics in homes, and during recreational activities. This increased consumption has led to high demand for fossil fuels and energy production. Subsequently, these natural resources have been over utilized resulting in their depletion.

Harmful Agricultural Practices
Agricultural activities have increased in most countries due to increasing demand for food. Some places clear out forests or use land inappropriately leading to the destruction of the environment. Additionally, large farms have been known to use harsh chemicals without proper disposal methods. This results in harmful products in the

soil and water. Therefore, agricultural activities are increasingly leading to the degradation of natural resources.

Conservation Of Natural Resources

In 1982, the United Nations saw the need for environmental protection and preservation of natural resources. The World Charter for Nature lists the measures to be taken to prevent depletion of natural resources. It also states the importance of environmental protection and the need to create laws on the same subject. Other organizations like the International Union for Conservation of Nature (IUCN) and the World Wide Fund for Nature (WWF) have also led in the push for protection of natural resources. The organizations have funded scientific studies like Conservation biology where scientists research on ways to conserve the natural resources found in the environment. At the local level, countries have established protected areas to conserve natural resources from exploitation. Conservationists also encourage the use of renewable natural resources such as wind and solar energy instead of non-renewable resources which are at risk of extinction. Additionally, most countries have government departments that oversee the extraction and use of natural resources. These departments create rules on management of natural resources like precious metals, rare metals, and energy sources. They also provide licenses to companies involved in the production and sale of such resources.

Why do we study resource economics?

Natural resource economics aims to study resources in order to prevent depletion. Natural resource utilization **is** regulated through the use of taxes and permits. The government and individual states determine how resources must be used and they monitor the availability and status of the resources

Is money an economic resource?

In economic terms, money is not a factor of production because it is a resource used to acquire resources that go into producing goods. The factors of production are capital, labor, and land.

What are entrepreneurship resources?

Entrepreneurial resources include sources of financing such as lines of credit and investment capital, but may also include abstract resources such as knowledge of a particular field or technology, or networks of contacts who can be called upon to contribute financial support, publicity, or other benefits.

What are land resources?

Land resources mean the resources available from the land, thus the agricultural land which contain natural fertilizer for growth of the products sown; the underground water, the various minerals like coal, gold and other raw materials.

Importance of Economic Resources

An economy is a system of institutions and organizations that either help facilitate or are directly involved in the production and distribution of goods and services. Economic resources are the inputs we use to produce and distribute goods and services. The precise proportion of each factor of production will vary from product to product and from service to service, and the goal is to make the most effective use of the resources that maximizes output at the least possible cost. Misallocation or improper use of resources may cause businesses, and even entire economies, to fail.

Depreciation

In Economics, depreciation is the gradual decrease in the economic value of the capital stock of a firm, nation or other entity, either through physical depreciation, obsolescence or changes in the demand for the services of the capital in question. If the capital stock is in one period, Gross investment spending on newly produced capital is and depreciation is, the capital stock in the next period, is . The net increment to the capital stock is the difference between gross investment and depreciation, and is called net investment The value of a capital asset may be modeled as the present value of the flow of services the asset will generate in future, appropriately adjusted for uncertainty. Economic depreciation over a given period is the reduction in the remaining value of future goods and services. Under certain circumstances, such as an unanticipated increase in the price of the services generated by an asset or a reduction in the discount rate, its value may increase rather than decline. Depreciation is then negative. Depreciation can alternatively be measured as the change in the market value of capital over a given period: the market price of the capital at the beginning of the period minus its market price at the end of the period. Depreciation = Total investment − net investment. Economic depreciation is different than accounting depreciation. In accounting depreciation, an asset is expensed over a specific amount of time, based on a set schedule.

How Economic Depreciation Works

Depreciation in economics is a measure of the amount of value an asset loses from influential factors affecting its market value. Asset owners may more closely consider economic depreciation over accounting depreciation if they seek to sell an asset at its market value.

Economic depreciation affects the selling value of an asset in the market. It may be followed and tracked by asset owners. In business accounting, economic depreciation is not typically notated on financial statement reporting for large capital assets since accountants usually use book value as the primary reporting method.

There can be several scenarios where economic depreciation is considered in financial analysis. Real estate is one of the most common examples but analysts may also consider it in other situations as well. Economic depreciation can also be a factor in forecasts of future revenues for goods and services.

Economic Depreciation vs. Accounting Depreciation

Calculating economic depreciation is not always as simple as in accounting depreciation. In accounting depreciation, a tangible asset's value decreases over time based on a set depreciation schedule. With economic depreciation an asset's decreases in value are not necessarily uniform or scheduled but rather based on influential economic factors.

Economic depreciation can often occur with real estate. In periods of economic downturn or a general housing market decline, economic depreciation may lead to a decrease in market value. The housing market environment can play a part in real estate valuations but individual valuations may also be affected by unfavorable neighborhood construction, road closures, a decline in the quality of a neighborhood, or other negative influences. Any type of negative economic factors can lead to economic depreciation and therefore a lower appraisal value. The difference in value from one appraisal to the next can show a property's economic depreciation.

Appraisals can be key to understanding economic depreciation. Appraisals can occur on all types of assets and are often the biggest determinant of economic depreciation.

Financial analysts may also consider economic depreciation when forecasting future projections and cash flows. Economic depreciation in these scenarios would be based on the decreases in the value of revenues expected from goods or services due to negative economic influences.

Accounting Depreciation

When people talk about depreciation, it is often in reference to accounting depreciation. Accounting depreciation is the process of allocating the cost of an asset over the course of its useful life so as to align its expenses with revenue generation. Businesses also create accounting depreciation schedules with tax benefits in mind since depreciation on assets is deductible as a business expense in accordance with the internal revenue service's (IRS) rules.

Most businesses depreciate an asset to $0 in book value because they believe the asset's value and expenses have been fully matched with the revenue it generates over its expected useful life. Companies may choose to hold some book value of a depreciated asset after it has been fully depreciated.

The book value of an asset and the market value of an asset are usually very different. The economic value or market value of an asset may not be reported on financial statements but it is the value a company could potentially get if they chose to make an asset sale.

References:

https://www.worldatlas.com/articles/what-are-natural-resources.html

https://en.m.wikipedia.org/wiki/Depreciation_(economics)
https://www.investopedia.com/terms/e/economicdepreciation.asp

Economic efficiency

The central economic problem is a scarcity of resources. It is very difficult to use, produce and distribute the resources in an efficient manner. Efficiency depends on productivity. The mathematical term of quality of economic products is,

$Q_{ep} = f(E)$ and $E = f(p_t)$
where, Q_{ep} = The quality of economic products,
E = efficiency and p_t = Productivity.
Productivity = Output per unit of input

The First Atom of the Universe

We know that according to the Big Bang concept, there was nothing except an super atom in the universe. Then anyhow the super atom was blasted and since then the observable universe is expanding. The observable universe is 13.5 billion years old and the earth is 4.5 billion years old. So the universe is three times older than the earth. But recently NASA has found a star which is about 16 billion years old. By this star's age it is proved that the creation time of visible universe is not true according to the Big Bang Concept. Suppose, the universe is a father and the recent finding star, Methusela or HD 140283, is a son. As a son can never be born before a father and everything has a center, I have firmly said that the Big Bang is a concept not a theory. I think, the universe is a big circle like our eye ball. As every circle has a center. So I firmly believe the Universe has a center. The universe is moving like a fan. All of the things has the definite uniform circular motion but different speed. Some think the sun is the center of our solar system. Some think the black hole of our milky way is the center. Some think that there is no center of the universe. There are more than one black holes in the universe and they are stars without shining power but super gravity. I think any star cannot be center of the universe. When I am trying to develop the Global Warming Macro Model a question came in my mind "Which is the center of the Universe?" I thought several times and watched nearly all videos about the universe on

Youtube Channel and read various articles but could not find any solution. Scientists, researchers, students of Astronomy believe that there is no center of the universe.

However, I have to find out where the first atom is. I think this is the point from where all the things of the universe get power to move their way like our navel point. Everything of the universe is dynamic. Some move round black holes. As black holes are a result of dying stars, black hole is not center. All things including black holes get circular power from the central point.

Now the question comes , " **How did the visible universe create ?**"

The Creator of the Universe knows well how He creates the universe. From the ancient time men have given many concepts about the universe. Of them the big bang is the most popular concept.

I think, once there was nothing except a super atom in the universe. This particle is very hot red colored. It moved very fast like a top. By spinning the atom created smoke and for spinning it was displacing slowly and created its own uniform circular axis way. This circular axis way is the center way of the universe. The smoke was gradually expanding and scattering various places in the universe. By gravity smoke of various places created planets, sub-planets, stars, comets, galaxies, local group galaxies etc. Everything has own uniform circular axis way for gravity. Dark matter creates gravity. Graviton particles are invisible. Various elements were concentrating the super atom slowly. As a result the atom was losing its flaming power gradually and becoming cool. These elements including the super atom created a planet. The interior part of this planet is very hot and the outer part has water, soil surrounding the super atom. The ratio of water and soil is about 2.45 : 1 . Of the whole water the purest drinkable water has near the super atom. This planet has CO_2O_2 cycle, a sub planet, animals, plants and aliens (visible and invisible). This is the only one planet whose has animals and aliens.

Center point theory

If the power of center point is zero, every thing of the universe will lose their circular and dynamic power and then universe is static that means time is zero. If it lasts few minutes all things lose their gravity, they will collide one another. The moon will lose its shining. As a result all the things of the area of the universe will destroy.

The Universe moves around the Holy First Particle of the Universe. Some think there is no center point in the universe. But think, without a central point how a circle is made. So without a center we cannot think about the universe. Stars, Solar system, star clusters, Galaxies, Galaxies clusters all have uniform circular motion. They move around the Holy First Atom. The universe has a center axis way. By this axis way a planet is moving. The planet has CO_2O_2 cycle and living beings. The Holy First Atom lies in the middle of the planet.

"The Universe is expanding "is a wrong idea. The things of the universe have a definite shape and a definite circular way and the dynamic power that comes from the central point of the Universe. To maintain balance they are dynamic and run their definite uniform circular axis. For this we see some planets or comets after every a long time. For example, Halley's comet appears in every 75 years. As everything of the universe is moving it seems to expand the universe. But really the universe is no expanding rather the number of the things is unchangeable.

The things can come to close one another according to their definite axis. They can not come out from their definite axis. If all things meet one another they will be a straight line. And the central point of the universe is in a middle position. Then we get the diameter of the universe. The diameter of the Universe is 254r billion light years. Here r is equal to 46.5 billion light years approximately. The angle of the straight line is 180°. But they do not collide one another because of wide space among them.

All the things of the universe move around the central point according to their own uniform circular motions. Central point is in the middle of a planet. This planet has CO_2O_2 cycle, animals and aliens. If the charging power of the central point is zero level, the universe is constant. As a result, there will be no motion in the universe. Surprisingly the central point gets charging power by human beings and invisible aliens.

Let's find out the first atom of the Universe. As every word of the Holy Quran is true, so we have to depend on the holy Quran. According to the Holy Quran the Universe consists of seven havens (skies) and made it in 6 cosmic days and also made the earth 2 cosmic days.

6 cosmic days / 2 cosmic days = 3

The verse number of Sura Al- Isra(The night journey) is 111

There are 3 pillars in the Kaba Sharif. The Kaba Sharif is the holiest place in the visible universe. The 3 pillars are situated just like 111. The 1st verse and 44th verse of the Sura Al- Isra are the symbol of the measurement, size ,position and center of the universe I think. Moreover, the 12th verse of this Sura is the symbol of the calculation of time, day, month and year.

1 cosmic day = 50000 years of the earth [According to the 4th verse of 70 Sura Mayariz]

86400 seconds of cosmic

= 50000 X 365 X 86400 seconds of the earth

1 cosmic second

= 50000 X 365 seconds of the earth

= 18250000 seconds of the earth

1 cosmic second = 211.227 days of the earth

1 cosmic second = 5470054250000 km

[since, speed of light = 299729 km / second]

1 cosmic second = $5.47005425 \times 10^{12}$ km

We know that ,

1 second of the earth = 299729 km

$= 2.99729 \times 10^5$ km

The difference between the cosmic second and earth second = 5470054250000 km - 299729 km

= 5470053950271 km

There are two special speeds in the universe. They are the speed of light and the speed of angel.

The speed of light = the speed of alien (Jinn)

= 299729 km per second

The speed of angel = 800 light year per second [Approx.]

The HOLY POINT is in the middle point of the Kaba Sharif which is at Mecca in Saudia Arabia. In the Kaba Sharif we see that there are three pillars. The Middle pillar is the center of the universe. The first atom of the universe is in this pillar. The big bang's point which is blasted for making the universe is there. Other two pillars has equidistant from the middle point. Man and Jinn move seven times around the Kaba Sharif. That means the universe is charged by human beings and jinn according to the Creator directions. As a result, all the things get charged to move their definite axis. If there is no man to move around the Kaba Sharif then the Universe will lose its circular motion power and the Universe will destroy. The day no man finds out to move the Kaba Sharif, that day the whole universe will be destroyed.

According to the Holy Quran, the beginning point (U_c) of the Universe is the middle pillar of the Kaba Sharif and the last point (U_L) of the Universe is Sidratul Muntaha. Kaba sharif has three pillars (1 - 1 - 1) . The verse number of Sura Al-Isra (The Night Journey) is 111. The Muslim have to move Seven times around the Kaba Sharif. As the Universe has seven heavens, the Muslim have to move seven times around the Kaba Sharif. I think, by moving 7 times around The Kaba Sharif human being charges the central point of the universe. This power goes all the things of the universe to get uniform circle motion. Rainbow has 7 colours and we know that white is made by 7 colours. The muslim when move around the Kaba Sharif they wear white coloured clothes. I think seven heavens, seven colours of rainbow and white colour of the Hazis' clothes have a connection.

1 and 44 verse of Sura Al-Isra (The Night Journey) of the Holy Quran are the source of my thought.

1 . " Glory to Him who journeyed his servant by night, from the Sacred Mosque to the Farthest Mosque, whose precincts We have blessed, in order to show him of Our wonders. He is the Listener, the Beholder."

Here, The Sacred Mosque means the Kaba Sharif. As the journey started from the Kaba Sharif, the center of the universe is the Kaba Sharif.

44. " Praising Him are the seven havens, and the earth and everyone . There is not a thing that does not glorify Him with praise, but you do not understand their praises. He is indeed Forbearing and Forgiving "

"The seven havens and the earth " is clue to measure the radius of the Universe. The center point is the middle pillar of Kaba Sharif. We see that the people who come to Makka in Soudi Arabia to say prayer all are moved seven times around the Kaba Sharif.

We cannot see the Creator but we believe and feel His existence everywhere. The Creator is One. He runs the whole universe.

Scientists cannot see the graviton particle but they believe that graviton particles have in the universe.

Therefore, I think the universe is not expanding , it is a circle and it has a central point and central axis. All the things of the Universe are moving around the middle pillar of the Kaba Sharif according to the uniform circular motion.

Calculation of the Radius and Area of the Universe

What we see with open eyes and with telescope is in the first sky (haven). They are a very little part of the radius of the first heaven. Stars, Solar system, Nebulae, star clusters, Galaxies, Galaxies clusters , black holes etc. are in the first circle . Consecutively diameter of one circle is the radius of other circle. That is, If the radius of the first circle is r , the diameter of the first circle (First haven) will be $2r$

. The diameter of the first circle is the radius of the second circle (the second). Continuously the radius of the seventh haven circle is the diameter of the sixth haven.

The radius of the Universe = 127r

$$\underset{\text{U}_\text{C} \hspace{5cm} \text{U}_\text{L}}{\overline{r(1+2+4+8+16+32+64)=127r}}$$

U_C is the central point and U_L is the last point of the universe

r = about 46.3 billion light years
The sum of seven circle's radius
= $(2^0 + 2^1 + 2^2 + 2^3 + 2^4 + 2^5 + 2^6) \, r$ billion light years
= $127 \, r$ billion light years

The circumference of the Universe
= $254 \, \pi \, r$ billion light years

The area of the Universe
= $\pi \, (127 \, r)^2$ square billion light years
= $16129 \pi r^2$ square billion light years
= $16129 \times 3.1416 \times (46.5)^2$ square billion light years
= $16129 \times 3.1416 \times 2162.25$ square billion light years [approx.]
= 109563080.8734 square billion light years [approx.]

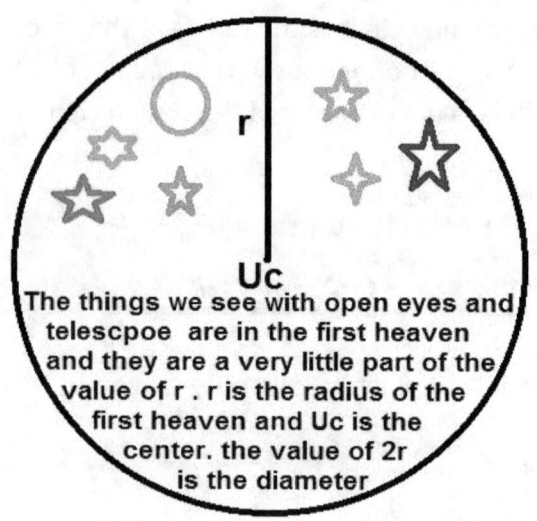

Figure: The First Heaven

r is the radius of the first heaven
Here, *r* = 46.5 billion light years [approx.]
$\quad\Pi$ = 3.1416

The diameter of the first heaven
= 2r
= (2 X 46.5) billion light years [approx.]
= 93 billion light years [approx.]

The circumference of the First Heaven
= 2 Π *r*
= 2 X 3.1416 X 46.5 billion light years [approx.]
= 292. 1688 billion light years [approx.]

The area of the first Heaven
= Πr^2
= 3.1416 X (46.5)² square billion light years
= 3.1416 X 2162.25 square billion light years
= 6792.9246 square billion light years

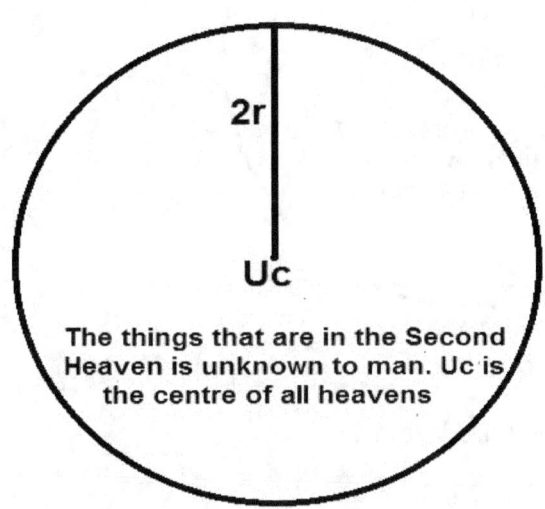

Figure: The Second Heaven

The circumference of the Second Heaven
= 4 Π r billion light years
= 4 X 3.1416 x 46.5 billion light years
= 584.3376 billion light years
The area of the Second Heaven
= $\Pi (2r)^2$ square billion light years
= $4\Pi r^2$ square billion light years

= 4 X 3.1416 X 2162.25 square billion light years
= 27171.6984 square billion light years

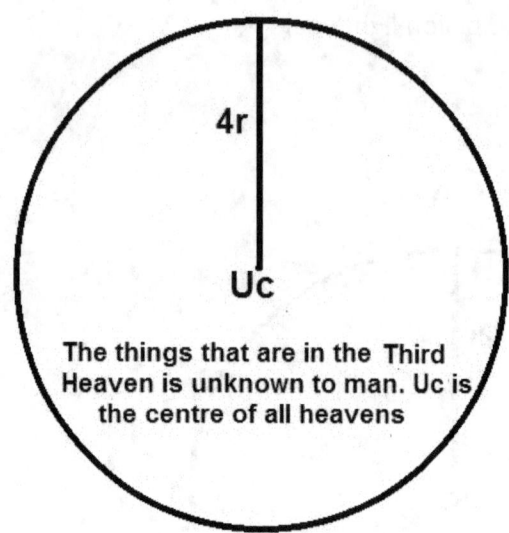

Figure: The Third Heaven

The radius of the third Heaven

= 4r = 4 X 46.5 billion light years

= 186 billion light years

The circumference of the Third Heaven
= 8 π r billion light years
= 8 X 3.1416 X 46.5 billion light years
= 1168.6752 billion light years
The area of the third Heaven
= $\pi (4r)^2$ square billion light years
= $16\pi r^2$ square billion light years
= 16 X 3.1416 X 2162.25 square billion light years

= 108686.7936 square billion light years

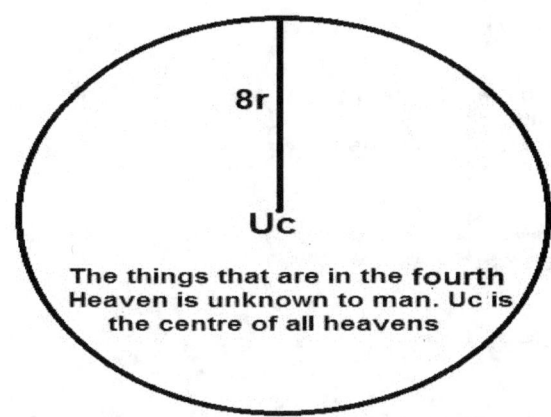

Figure: The Fourth Heaven

The radius of the fourth heaven

= 8r = 8 X 46.5 billion light years

= 372 billion light years

The circumference of the fourth Heaven
= 16 π r billion light years
= 16 X 3.1416 X 46.5 billion light years
= 2337.3504 billion light years

The area of the fourth Heaven
= $\pi (8r)^2$ square billion light years
= $64\pi r^2$ square billion light years
= 64 X 3.1416 X 2162.25 square billion light years
= 434747.1744 square billion light years

Figure: The 5th Heaven

The radius of the 5th heaven
= 16r
= 16 X 46.5 billion light years
= 744 billion light years

The circumference of the 5th Heaven
= 32 π r billion light years
= 32 X 3.1416 X 46.5 billion light years
= 4674.7008 billion light years

The area of the 5th Heaven
= $\pi (16r)^2$ square billion light years
= $256\pi r^2$ square billion light years
= 256 X 3.1416 X 2162.25 square billion light years
= 1738988.6976 square billion light years

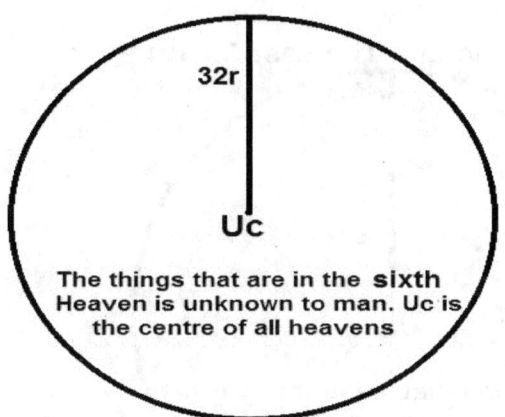

Figure: The Sixth Heaven

32r is the radius of the sixth heaven

The circumference of the sixth Heaven
= 64 π r billion light years
= 64 X 3.1416 X 46.5   billion light years
= 9349.4016   billion light years

The area of the sixth Heaven
= π $(32r)^2$ square billion light years
= $1024πr^2$ square billion light years
= 1024 X 3.1416 X 2162.25 square billion light years
= 6955954.7904 square billion light years

Sidratul Muntaha The Last Creature

```
         SM
        |
      64r
        |
       Uc
```

The things that are in the **seventh** Heaven is unknown to man. Uc is the centre of all heavens
SM = Sidratul Muntaha

Figure: The Seventh Heaven

The radius of the seventh heaven
= 64r
= 64 X 46.5 billion light years
= 2976 billion light years

The circumference of the seventh Heaven
= 128 π r billion light years
= 128 X 3.1416 X 46.5 billion light years
= 18698.8032 billion light years

The area of the seventh Heaven
= $\pi (64r)^2$ square billion light years
= $4096 \pi r^2$ square billion light years
= 4096 X 3.1416 X 2162.25 square billion light years
= 27823819.1616 square billion light years

The sum of seven circle's radius
= $(2^0 + 2^1 + 2^2 + 2^3 + 2^4 + 2^5 + 2^6)$ r billion light years
= 127 r billion light years
= 127 X 46.5 billion light years [Approximately]
= 5905.5 billion light years [Approximately]
So the Radius of the Universe is almost 5905.5 billion light years [Approximately].

The area of the universe
= $\pi (127r)^2$ square billion light years
= $16129 \pi r^2$ square billion light years
= 16129 X 3.1416 X 2162.25 square billion light years
= 109563080.8734 square billion light years [Approx.]

Position of the Creator

= $(16129 \pi r^2 + X^2)$ square billion light years

= $(109563080.8734 + X^2)$ square billion light years [approx.]

All the things of the area of $16129 \pi r^2$ square billion light years (approximately) will be destroyed on the last day of the Universe by the One who occurred the big bang.

When the charging power of the central point is Zero. All the things in the area of the Universe will destroy. Only The Creator is and will be remain everywhere.

Location of Angels, Aliens and Animals

Nowadays the word Alien is the most talked of topic in the world. Children are very interested to know about alien instead of ghost or fairy. Space crafts are sent one planet to another planet for finding out Alien. Still now science has failed to discover alien. Some scientists believe that there is life beyond the earth. For this they send rockets to another planet from the earth. Still now they have failed to discover the location of Alien. The picture of alien we see is not true. It is an unreal image. I think aliens live with us since the first man. There are two speedy creatures in the universe. Their speeds are faster than man-made vehicle's speed. human being can not see them. These two creature of the universe are angels and aliens. Here I would like to discuss about angels, aliens and animals and theory of travelling time in the universe and the fastest speed particle in the universe which is more speed than the light speed.

Angels

The graviton particles of the universe are not seen but we feel that there is a dark energy between two planets. Same way angels are not seen but we feel their existence invisibly. The other name of graviton particles is angel's particle. Dark matter and dark energy related to angles. Angels live everywhere in the universe. They can change their physical form. They are visible but due to the fastest speed in the Universe we , human beings, can not see them. Angel's speed per second is the distance that from the earth to the Rigel [approximately]. The distance from the earth to the Rigel is 800 light years. So Angel speed is about 800 light years per second. Their actual size and form is so gigantic that we cannot imagine it. Angles have many wings which help them fly faster than most other speed medias. The honest and innocent great men can see them.

Luckily, in the seventh century the most honest and innocent great man of the earth travelled the Universe with angle's speed one night. Duration of his journey was only a small part of that night. It is possible because of the help of angel speed. From his journey we learn that the last creature of the universe is The Sidratul Muntaha. The Sidratul Muntaha is a kind of tree.

Aliens

This is a concept that alien may exist beyond the earth. But we don't know that aliens live with us from the first human being. The modern name of Jinn is Alien. Jinn have two wings and move one place to another at the light speed which is 299729 km per second , invisible and sometimes visible but holding various forms. Most of the jinn come to human beings and live together invisibly. They can change their visible shape like as a chameleon changes its colour. There are two kinds of alien in the universe. One type is related jinn .The worst jinn and his fellow eat animals' blood and things of dustbin. They like to change original shape into snakes. The worst jinn or alien whom we call the devil lives in the middle of the Bermuda Triangle. The place is in the western part of the

Atlantic Ocean. The top point of the Bermuda Triangle is Bermuda and other two points are Miami and Puerto Rico. From there the worst jinn connects its fellow jinns and the successors of the worst jinn. Most of the successors are involved in homosexual, sucking human blood, creating quarrelling among human beings. Bad jinns love to the individuals who practice gambling, suicide, homosexuality etc.

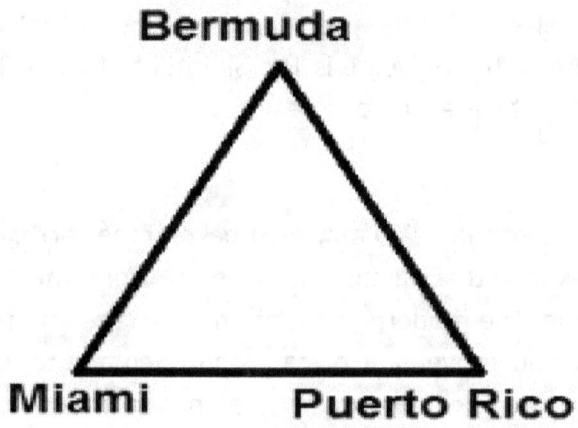

On the other hand, the best alien and his fellow live in the Jinn hill of Saudi Arabia and various places where people normally do not go or stay. Female jinn is called fairy. Jinn can travel any place with the speed of light. Sometimes we hear that someone of us has seen the Jinn and Fairy. Someone of us brings them up. They travel in the universe at night. From the earth they reach the moon within 1.28

second. Every night they travel one planet to other planet within a few moments. The honest jinn fellow love to eat sweets.

Another type is human-formed alien. Human–formed alien's fore parents were the worst Jinn and an Egyptian woman. Once human-formed aliens ruled Egypt. They were called Pharaoh. They are visible but the worst Jinn and his fellow jinn can not be seen.
Human-formed aliens are identified very easy. They love Pyramid because their predecessors were buried there and like to show sign of triangle various motions, one eye in a triangle. About 6000 years ago, in Egypt this type of aliens were born and gradually live with human beings. One night when the worst jinn, the Satan, travelled in the universe, he saw an unclean woman in Egypt. In guise of human being he came to the woman and stayed the whole night with her. After ten months she gave birth the first human-formed alien. When the son was adult, he would rape, lend gold with interest, do homosexuality, make people fool by telling lies and cheat for capturing his interest. Very often the worst jinn came to that man. Son of the worst jinn, the first human-formed alien, became the father of many human-formed aliens. He made friendship with the royal officials to meet the king of Egypt. Several times he lent gold to the royal officials to manage them in his need. Managing all of the royal officials once he killed the king and declared the king of Egypt . All royal officials obeyed to him because every royal officials borrowed a lot of gold to him. They carried out human-formed alien lest they should repay the loan

with high interest. Gradually the first human-formed successors spread their characters all over the world. At first they spread loan business. Gradually Banking system established.

I think , at present about 10 billion human-formed aliens live all over the world especially Israel, the USA, Australia, England, Germany, France, Austria, Japan, Chine, Mongolia, Brazil, India etc. For the conspiracy of human-formed alien the French revolution and Russian revolution occurred, British East India Company are forced to collect tax from the people of sub continental, the world war I and II happened, banking system spread and many political leaders of the world were killed. Nowadays most of the successors of the first human-formed alien's blood line live in the US. I respect John F Kennedy, the 35th President of the US, who wanted to free The US from human-formed aliens. But he was killed by the helper of aliens. Maybe the 41st and 43rd Presidents of the US are human-formed aliens. Because of their wrong decisions, people all over the world had been suffering many economical problems.

If the 43rd President, George W. Bush's DNA is tested and checked with the dead body of the Pharaoh which is in the Cairo Museum, it will be cleared whether Mr. Bush is alien or not. Only for establishing NEW WORLD ORDER the world trade center was damaged on 11 September 2001 through the conspiracy of alien Mr. Bush. Only for oil he attacked Iraq on the basis of false news. For Mr. Bush's guilty many innocent of Iraqi people were killed, raped and tortured. Only for Mr. Bush's wrong decision Euro crisis occurred and Spain, France, Greece faced economical difficulty, Iraqi and Afghanistani innocent people were killed and independent countries were attacked. These are not the behaviors of a human being like Mr. Bush. When Adlof Hitler came to learn that there were some human-formed aliens in Jew, without justifying aliens he decided to kill Jews at random during the World War II. But it was his guilty to kill innocent people of Jew. I think, George W. Bush is more hatred person than Adlof Hitler. Israel often attacks Palestine and kills a number of innocent people including babies, women to capture land. And we see that Human Rights Organizations remain silent. I think aliens run the human rights organizations because aliens do not understand humanity and they only know how to decrease the number of human beings. Moreover, Princess Diana and Michael Jackson were killed by the conspiracy of Aliens.

Homosexuality is one of the most identified features of the human-formed aliens. Mr. Barak Obama supported it. That means he is involved in homosexuality. The persons who practices this bad habit are sick or human-formed aliens. They want to decrease the number of human beings. It is a prerequisite condition of aliens. Aliens want to kill human beings. For this reason they encourage individuals who kill spam, do abortion and suicide, sex with others spouses and divorce etc. Aliens do not want to see husband-wife harmony. It is a matter of sorrow that aliens capture the mass media of the world by their gold power. Indirectly they are investing in the films of the Hollywood, Bollywood and so on and video songs of the famous singers for advertising their pyramid sign, one eye, two horns through fingers.

Animals
Human beings and other animals live only in the earth. Without the earth no animal can live in other planet because of CO_2O_2 cycle and the distance from the sun. There is no CO_2O_2 cycle in the universe except the earth. We, Human beings, can never naturally change physical form. We can travel any space according to our scientists' made vehicle's speed. According to the Scientist Albert Einstein we cannot travel with the speed of light. But I think if we make friendship with jinn, we can travel one planet to another planet with jinn's speed.

Theory of Travelling Time in the Universe

Everything in the universe is moving. Everything has definite speed, gravity and axis way. The universe seems to expand. It seems because all things are moving with their own unique speeds. There are no two things which have same speed in the universe. The moon is used for the counting months and the sun is used for the counting years in the context of the earth. We see day night because of the earth's spinning.

To reach any planet from the earth if media of speed is more than the speed of light, it will take less time than that of light speed. Inversely it will take more time than that of light speed.

Here, Universe travelling time is equal to the product of Three quantities. They are the distance from the earth, speed media and the constant of travelling universe.
That is,
$T_t = c^{-2}DS$ seconds $= DS/c^2$ seconds
Where, T_t = time of travelling planet
c^{-2} = Constant of travelling universe
D = Distance from the earth
S = media of speed
c = 299729 km/second = speed of Alien = speed of light

$c^2 = (299729)^2 = 89837473441 = 8.9837473441 \times 10^{10}$
Constant of the travelling Universe
$= c^{-2} = 1/c^2 = 1/(8.9837473441 \times 10^{10})$
$= (1/8.9837473441) \times (1/10000000000)$
$= 0.1113121241835392368511878840 2058 \times 0.0000000001$
$= 0.00000000001113121241835392368 5118788402058$

There are several media of speed in the universe.
Jinn or alien speed (Light speed) = c = 299792 km / second
Angel speed = as far as we see / second [approx.]
Human made various speeds
      i)   Rocket speed
      ii)   Plane speed
      iii)   Train speed
      iv)   Bus speed
      v)   Car speed
      vi)   Running speed
      vii)   Walking speed
Various animals have various speed.

Here, Angel speed > Jinn speed > Human made media's speed > running speed > walking speed

According to Einstein's Theory of Relativity, there is an unimaginable difference between the time value of the earth and the time value of beyond the earth.

1 day of the earth = 86400 seconds and c = 299792 km/second

50000 years of the earth = 50000 X 365 X 86400 seconds
= 50000 X 365 X 86400 X 299792 km
= 472712025600000000 km
=(472712025600000000 / 9452253744000) light year

We know that,
Unit of time is second
1 minute = 60 seconds
1 hour = 60 minutes = (60 X 60) seconds
= 3600 seconds
1 day = 24 hours = (24 X 3600) seconds
= 86400 seconds

1 month = 30 days = (30 X 86400) seconds
= 2592000 s

1 year = 365 days = 86400 X 365 seconds
= 31536000 seconds
1 light year = 31536000 X 299729 km
= 9452253744000 km
800 light year = 800 X 9452253744000 km
= 7561802995200000 km

To sum up,
Alien speed = speed of light = c = 299729km/ second

Angel speed =7561802995200000 km / second [approx.]
Constant of the travelling Universe = c^{-2} = 1 /c^2
Tt = c^{-2}DS seconds
Therefore, in the universe angel speed is the fastest speed of all things.

Theory of the Global Warming

At present the global warming and climate change is the most talked topic in the world. We know that global warming means the increasing average global temperature. Various scientists and researchers give the reasons, effects and probable solution of this global problem in literature manner. Recently a scientist has said that the earth is closing to the sun. For this the temperature of the earth is increasing. But no scientist or researcher develop a theory of global warming and climate change. It is I who am a student of welfare economic system since 2013 and practitioner Ecophysics (Economics + Physics) making a mathematical model for the global warming. By this model we can calculate the global warming, calculate the amount CO_2, minimize the amount CO_2 (Carbon dioxide) for the green world, determine the amount of other greenhouse gases, how many trees will need to remove global warming, determine the time when we will get the dreamy healthy world and find out the time when we control the weather of the world.

I have calculated one degree Celsius global warming is equal to (*48184380 + a*) kiloton CO_2 and one kiloton CO_2 is *equal to 5.42 kiloton O_2 in the context of absorbing by a tree.* **One degree Celsius Global warming is equal to $66.02328T^{-1}$ degree adjacent angle**. In micro sense I have made the Global Warming Micro Model and then in macro sense I have established the Global Warming Macro Model. I believe that men have the power to control the weather of the world. It is our sacred duty to protect other animals and look after the earth like our sweet homes.

I think today's world is like a poor debt family in CO_2O_2 cycle. If CO_2 is Expenditure and O_2 (Oxygen) is income then the world's income (O_2) is less than CO_2. This is a problem and the problem is too large for us to imagine it.

In order to develop this model I have used velocity, acceleration and differential. In micro sense, to solve the problem we have to increase O_2 and at the same time we have to minimize CO_2. In macro sense, we have to minimize greenhouse gases (CH_4, N_2O and other green house gases) like compound interest loan and also minimize thermal energy which created by friction. This thermal energy is always ignored by scientists and researchers. I think this is a small matter but significantly big problem.

Fundamental Concepts of Global Warming Model

Global warming depends on the proportion of two groups elements. They are the increasing elements and the decreasing elements. The increasing elements are CO_2, CH_4 (Methane) , Nitrous Oxide(N_2O) and other greenhouse gases. The decreasing elements are O_2 and human's propensity to save the earth. **If the value of proportion of two groups is more than one, the global warming**

increases and if the value of the proportion is less than one, the global warming decreases.

The relationship between the global warming and the increasing elements (CO_2 and other GHG) is positive but there is negative relationship between the global warming and the decreasing element (O_2). Oxygen is only hero elements to protect the earth like a hero protects a heroine from evils. As trees can absorb CO_2 which is the most responsible element for global warming and release O_2 for animals living. Besides, more than sufficient trees can help human beings control CH_4, Nitrous Oxide and other greenhouse gases. So I concentrate on CO_2O_2 cycle which is not found any other planet I think. Many scientists believe that after 2030 many animals will be extincting for global warming. So it is important to know how much O_2 require against global warming and climate change, how much CO_2 should minimize from atmosphere to save the world, how many trees should have for living in the world, how to control weather for protecting against natural disasters. It is high time we did something for protecting animals including human beings from extinction. I am trying to save the loving world by developing theory, promoting it all over the world to apply it for the peaceful world of our next generation.

Global Warming Micro Model

" The more the value of the proportion of the efficiency of CO_2 emissions and the efficiency of O_2 production increases, the more the value of multiplier of global warming will increase and inversely decrease. When the value of the proportion is one, the Average Global

Temperature will be constant in the context of CO_2O_2 cycle."

$w = c\,(x)^{-1}$ where, $c > 0$, $x > 0$ and if $w > 1$ then the global warming exists

$\theta = w\,(90/100)$ degree adjacent angle

Gw = Global warming = $\theta / 66.02328 T^{-1}$ °C

GW indicates the Average Global Temperature or Global Warming
c = the efficiency of CO_2 emissions
$= (CO_2\,f - CO_2\,i) / CO_2\,f$
$= \Delta CO_2 / CO_2$ [$CO_2 f$ = final CO_2 and $CO_2\,i$ = initial CO_2]
x = the efficiency of O_2 production
$= (O_2\,f - O_2\,i) / O_2\,f$
$= \Delta O_2 / O_2$ [$O_2 f$ = final O_2 and $O_2\,i$ = initial O_2]
we get c by burning fossil fuels (i.g. coal, oil and gas) and x by planting trees and the number of trees in this world.
In global warming level $c > x$. The world people face this great problem now.

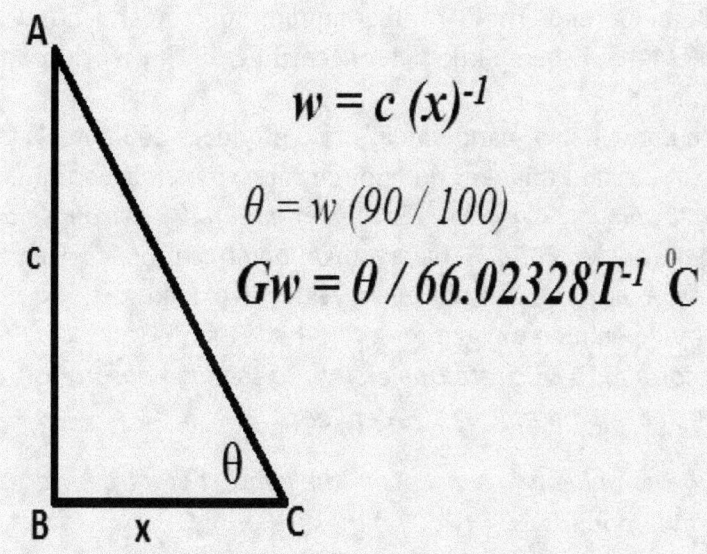

Figure: Global Warming Micro Model

In the figure, ABC is a right angled Triangle. Angle ABC = 90°, Angle ACB = θ, AB = perpendicular, BC = Base and
AC = Hypotenuse. By increasing BC the value of θ will decrease. As a result the global warming will decrease.
In 2013 the amount of CO_2 = CO_2i was 35837591 kiloton and 1n 2014 the amount of CO_2= CO_2f was 36138285 kiloton according to The World Bank Data Group.
c = (36138285 − 35837591) kt / 36138285 kt
  = 300694 kt / 36138285 kt
  = 0.00839046 kt
Therefore, $c = \Delta CO_2 / CO_2$ = 0.00839046 kt

In 2013 the amount of forest land was 40057482 square kilometer and 1n 2014 the amount of forest land was 40024403.3 square kilometer according to The World Bank Data Group.

We know that a matured leafy tree produces 260 pounds O_2 in a year and this will do enough for two men according to *Environment Canada, Canada's national environmental agency. They said,"* "On average, one tree produces nearly 260 pounds of oxygen each year. Two mature trees can provide enough oxygen for a family of four."

According to NC State University, "a tree can absorb as much as 48 pounds of CO_2 per year."

If we combine two concepts in the context of a tree, we get, 48 pounds CO_2 = 260 pounds O_2
1 pound CO_2 = (260 / 48)pounds O_2
= 5.42 pounds O_2 [approximately]
Therefore, 1 kiloton CO_2 = 5.42 kiloton O_2 [approximately]
That is, If we want to remove 1 kt CO_2, we need 5.42 kt O_2. [appr.]

Suppose, T matured leafy trees are in one square kilometer
In one square kilometer,
T produces $(260 * T)/ 2204.6$ kt O_2 [since 1ton = 2204.6 pounds]
$= 0.12T$ ton O_2
So, one square kilometer forest land produces $0.12T$ kt O_2
In 2013 the world produced the amount of $O_2 = O_2i$
$= 40057482 * 0.12T$ ton O_2
$= 4806897.84T$ ton O_2
$= 4806897.84T / 1000$ kt O_2 [since 1 kiloton = 1000 ton]
$= 4806.89784T$ kt O_2
In 2014 the world produced the amount of $O_2 = O_2f$
$= 40024403.3 * 0.12T$ ton $O2$

$= 4802928.396\ T\ ton\ O_2$
$= 4802928.396\ T / 1000\ kt\ O_2$ [since 1 kiloton $= 1000$ ton]
$= 4802.928396T\ kt\ O_2$
$\Delta O_2 = (4802.928396T - 4806.89784T)\ kt\ O_2$
    $= -3.969444T\ kt\ O_2$

To save the earth for existing of animals we should increase the amount of oxygen but we cut down trees for our comfortable in exchange of our slowly but surely dead of our future generation.

Negative value of ΔO_2 is the evidence of that word.
Avoiding negative sign we get $\Delta O_2 = 3.969444\ kt$
$x = 3.969444T / 4802.928396T\ kt\ O_2$
  $= 3.97T / 4802.93\ T\ kt\ O_2$
  $= 0.00082658T\ kt\ O_2$
  $= 0.00082658T\ kt / 5.42\ kt\ CO_2$ [appr.] [since, $1kt\ CO_2 = 5.42\ kt\ O_2$]
  $= 0.0001525T\ kt\ CO_2$

We, the inhabitants of the earth, make $c = 0.00839046\ kt\ CO_2$
and $x = 0.0001525T\ kt\ CO_2$ [approximately]

We have to increase the value of x more than c. But we have increased c more than necessity. As a result, the extinction of animals including human beings count down.

$w = c/x = 0.00839046\ kt\ CO_2 / 0.0001525T\ kt\ CO_2$
$= \mathbf{55.0194T^{-1}\ kt\ CO_2}$
$w = 55.0194T^{-1} * 90\ degree / 100$
$= 49.51746T^{-1}\ degree\ adjacent\ angle$

According to NASA in 2014 the global temperature was 0.75 degree Celsius
0.75 degree Celsius global warming $= 49.51746T^{-1}$ degree adjacent angle
Or, 1 degree Celsius global warming

$= 49.51746T^{-1}$ degree adjacent angle $/ 0.75$
$= 66.02328T^{-1}$ degree adjacent angle

So, one degree Celsius Global warming $= 66.02328T^{-1}$ degree adjacent angle

When the value of adjacent angle is one, we get the balance of $CO_2 O_2$

The more the value of w increases, the more the earth will unsuitable for living place and the more animal will extinct.
In balance level, $c / x = 1$
Or, $\Delta CO_2 / \Delta O_2 = 1$
Or, $\Delta CO_2 = \Delta O_2$
If ΔCO_2 is not equals to ΔO_2, it means it does not establish balance.
If ΔCO_2 is greater than ΔO_2, it means there is global warming.
If ΔCO_2 is smaller than ΔO_2, it means the earth is suitable for animals.

The velocity of Gw is increasing because the velocity of ΔCO_2 is increasing and the velocity of ΔO_2 is decreasing. As a result, the velocity of ΔCO_2 is more than the velocity of ΔO_2 and the velocity of VGw is increasing That is,
$VGw = (Gwf - Gwi) / Time$,
$V\Delta CO_2 = (\Delta CO_2 f - \Delta CO_2 i) / Time$
$V\Delta O_2 = (\Delta O_2 f - \Delta O_2 i) / Time$
Therefore, $VGw = V\Delta CO_2 / V\Delta O_2$
the acceleration of Gw is a non-uniform acceleration because the value of CO_2, O_2 and other greenhouse gases are variable.

In my global warming micro model I would not like to discuss the other Greenhouse gases such as Nitrous Oxide (N_2O), Mithene (CH_4), Chlorofluorocarbon (CFC_{12}), Hydrofluorocarbon-23 (HFC_{23}), Sulfer Hexa Fluoride (SF_6), Nitrozen Trifluoride (NF_3) because O_2 can not absorb these gases but by increasing O_2 it may reduce other greenhouse gases. So we have to minimize CO_2 on the priority basis.

According to NASA,
In 2014 Average Global Temperature (Gw) = 0.75 degree Celsius
Average Global Temperature in 2000 according to NASA
= 0.40 degree Celsius
The velocity of global warming from 2000 to 2014
= (0.75 – 0.40) / 14
= 0.025 degree Celsius
The velocity of CO_2 from 2000 to 2014

= (36138285 kt – 24689911 kt) / 14

= 817741 kty^{-1}

The velocity of forest land from 2000 to 2014

= (40024403.3 km^2 - 40556022.3 km^2) / 14

= - 37972.786 km^{2}y^{-1}

Every year we lose approximately 37972.786 km^{2}y^{-1} forest land
Avoiding negative sign we get ,

the velocity of forest land is 37972.786 km^{2}y^{-1} .

Every year we lose approximately 37972.786 km^{2}y^{-1} forest land.

To manage deficit O_2,
We have to plant more trees.
We have to use renewable energy.
We have to avoid furniture made of wood.

Government should take Carbon tax from the factories which use fossil fuels and the individual who uses fossil fuel for driving personal car.

After managing deficit O_2 within 20 years we will reach the green world, I think. But we have not sufficient time to turn our beloved world into the green world within 20 years. We, the inhabitants of the world, are not united for minimizing carbon dioxide and increasing tree plantation. The United Nations sometimes fails to establish harmony between two conflict countries. Sometimes the United Nations remains silent to control the capitalist. However, We, the inhabitants of the earth, may vary from colour to colour, race to race, religion to religion but we all can unite for saving the world against global warming and climate change. To protect the earth against global warming we have to work unitedly by applying this theory, I think.

Calculation of how much CO_2 is responsible for *n* degree global warming

According to NASA in 2014,
 the Average Global Temperature was 0.75 degree Celsius
And according to the World Bank Carbon emissions was 36138285 kiloton
So, we get,
0.75 degree Celsius Gw = 36138285 kiloton CO_2 + GHGo

Or, 1 degree Celsius Gw = (36138285 kt CO_2 + GHGo) / 0.75

Or, 1 °C Gw = (36138285 kt CO_2 / 0.75) + (GHGo / 0.75)

Or, 1 °C Gw = 48184380 kt co_2 + a
[let, a = GHGo / 0.75]

As O_2 can absorb CO_2. a can be minimized by human behaviors. So in micro sense, Global warming multiplier depends on the proportion of c and x

One degree Celsius Global Warming is equal to
48184380 kt CO_2 + a

2 °C GW = 96368760 kt CO_2 + 2a

n °C GW = n (48184380 kt CO_2 + a)

The Global Warming Macro Model

In macro sense, the Creator gives human beings the power to control the atmosphere because everything of the universe is made for human beings. Global Warming depends on human activities. Two types of coefficients are created by human activities . they are increasing elements of global warming and decreasing elements of global warming.

If the proportion of the sum of the marginal propensity of increasing elements is equal to the sum of the

marginal propensity of decreasing elements, the changing rate of Global Warming will be constant and establish the green world.

The global warming Macro function,
$GW = f(P) = f(CO_2, O_2, Re, GHGo, AntiGHGo, TEc)$
Where, GW = Global Warming, P = Population, CO_2 = Carbon dioxide, O_2 = Oxygen, Re = Renewable Energy, GHGo = CH_4, N_2O and other greenhouse gases, TEc = Thermal Energy caused by friction, AntiGHGo = Action against GHGo
$GW = f(P) = hP$
Therefore, $dGW/dP = h > 0$
where, P = Population of the world, h = the marginal propensity of human being's behavior
The global warming macro equation,
$GW = f(CO_2) + f(GHGo) - f(O_2) - f(Re) - f(AntiGHGo) + f(TEc)$
Part of $GW = f(CO_2) = kCO_2$
Therefore, $dGW/dCO_2 = k > 0$
Where, c = the marginal propensity of CO_2 emissions

Part of $GW = f(O_2) = -sO_2$
Therefore, $dGW/dO_2 = -s < 0$
Where, x = the marginal propensity of O_2

Part of $GW = f(Re) = -rRE$
Therefore, $dGW/dRE = -r < 0$
Where, r = the marginal propensity of using Renewable Energy

Part of $GW = f(GHGo) = g\ GHGo$
Therefore, $dGW/dGHGo = g > 0$
Where, g = the marginal propensity of other greenhouse gases

Part of GW = f (Tec) = e TEc
Therefore, dGW / dTEc = e > 0

Part of GW = f (AntiGHGo) = - y AntiGHGo
Therefore, dGW/ dAntiGHGo = - y < 0
Where, y = the marginal propensity of antiGHGo

The global warming macro equation,
  $GW = k\ CO_2 + g\ GHGo - s\ O_2 - r\ Re - y\ AntiGHGo + e\ Tec$
Or, $\Delta GW / \Delta (CO_2+O_2+Re+GHGo+ AntiGHGo + TEc) = k + g - s - r - y + e$
    Or, $\Delta GW / \Delta P = h = \tan\theta$
If h = 45 degree then there will establish ecological balance
But it is a matter of sorrow that today's world face h = $\tan\theta$ > 45 degree . For this reason we face global warming.

When h = $\tan\theta$ = 45 degree, then *(k+g+ e) / (r+s+y) = 1*
When, $\tan\theta$ > 45 dgree, then *(k+g+e) / (r + s + y) > 1*
When, $\tan\theta$ < 45 dgree, then *(k+g+e) / (r + s + y)   < 1*

Here, *(k + g + e)* is the sum of k,g and e
      (r + s + y) is the sum of r,s and y
So we all, the people of the world, have to work for increasing the value of (r + s + y) and decreasing the value of (k + g + e).
Now the world faces the following diagram,

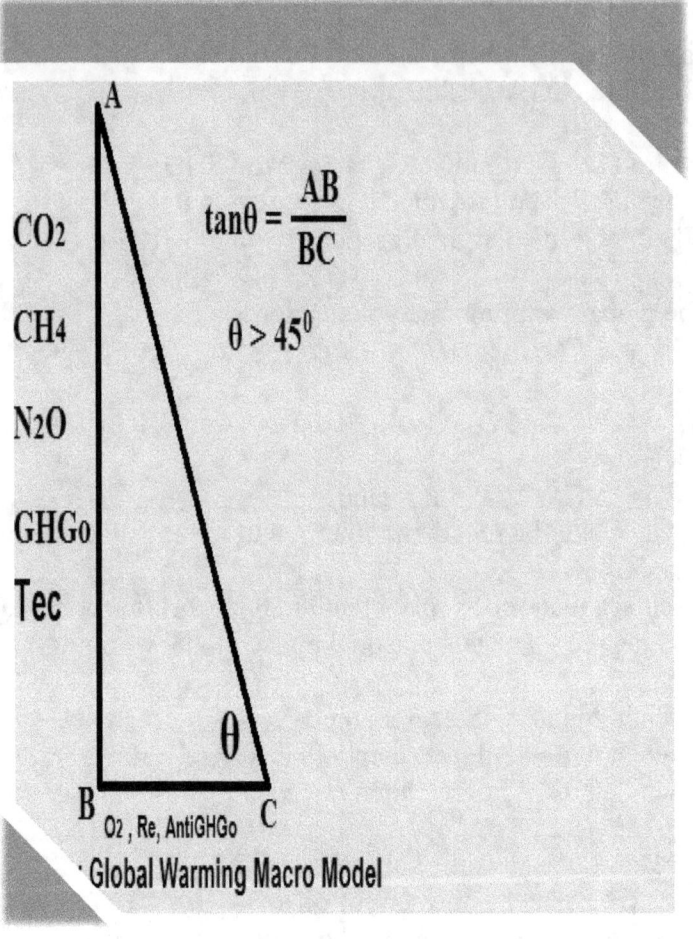

Global Warming Macro Model

In the figure, ABC is a right angled triangle. Angle ABC = 90°,
angle ACB = θ
AB / BC = $\tan\theta$ = h = (k + g + e) / (r + s + y)

The 21th century of people face the gigantic problem which is called the global warming. For the global warming the world people are seeing how sea water level is increasing, polar ice is melting, many islands is sinking, many animals are disappearing and seeing various natural disasters. Suppose, you want to boil a kettle of water by heating. What will happen when the water of the kettle boils ? You can see that water level of the kettle is rising. Like the kettle our earth is heating by burning fossil fuels, using fertilizer and using various types of glass for building high rise tower, using automobiles .This heat is the main cause of increasing global temperature and increasing sea water level. When water heats up, it increases. So when the ocean warms, sea level rises. Polar ice is melting for global warming and water created by melting water runs into the ocean and thus sea water is rising gradually and it helps methane (CH4) emit.

Many of us believe that many islands around the world are slowly but surely submerged by 2050 because of rising sea water level. This will happen only for global warming.

Some Functions for Global Warming

According to the macro model, there are some functions for global warming. I would like to discuss these functions. The first function is called carbon dioxide - global warming function.

The carbon dioxide – global warming function

Global warming depends on mainly CO_2. There are positive relationship between G_w and CO_2.
The more CO_2 increases the more global warming increases and inversely decreases.
G_w is dependent variable and CO_2 is an independent variable.
So the function is,

$Gw = f(CO_2)$
The equation of the global warming – carbon dioxide is,
$Gw = k\ CO_2$
Therefore, $\Delta Gw / \Delta CO_2 = k$

The Global Warming-Oxygen Function

There is an inverse relationship between Gw and O_2. The more the amount of oxygen increases the more the amount of Gw decreases.

The function of global warming – Oxygen is,

$Gw = f(O_2) = -s\ O_2$

Therefore, $\Delta Gw / \Delta O_2 = -s$

To minimize global warming we have to increase the quantity of forest land. Trees take CO_2 and give O_2 to maintain ecological balance. But at present the lower amount of O_2 do not perfectly absorb the higher amount of CO_2 because of human activities. We have to plant trees here and there where we find open space I think every man needs at least 226 trees to exist in the world. So we have to plant at least 226 trees per capita. By planting trees we can save many human lives and wild lives and maintain ecological balance.

The function of Carbon dioxide minimization in atmosphere by O_2

Naturally 5.42 unit oxygen is equal to 1 unit CO_2.
$$CO_2 = f(O_2) = t\ O_2$$
Or, $CO_2 / t = O_2$
Or, $CO_2\ (t)^{-1} = O_2$
Or, $(t)^{-1} = O_2 / CO_2$

Since, $CO_2 > O_2$ and in global warming level CO_2 is positive
By planting trees we will get $t = 5.42$
When we get $t = 5.42$, we will minimize $CO2$
At present t is less than 5.42. We have to face natural disasters and climate change.
The G7 (Group of Seven) countries like USA, Canada, Japan, England, France, Germany, Italy and developing counties like Chine, Brazil, India, Australia , Rasia etc use fossil fuels (i.e. coal, oil, natural gas) for increasing GNI (Gross National Income) and produce a large number of Carbon dioxide which is responsible for climate change. Most of them are unwilling to reduce the use of fossil fuels.

Due to deforestation the present number of trees can not normally absorb CO_2 from the air. If we have to eat 50 kilogram rice without any time interval, what will happen ? Just imagine. Same condition exists for the number trees of the world in the context of absorbing CO_2. Rather trees lose their normal power to absorb CO_2 and release poor oxygen.

Renewable Energy- Global Warming Function

The more the users of renewable energy increase, the more the global warming decrease. There is a negative relationship between Re and Gw. We have to use renewal energy i.g. hydro power, biomass, solar panel, wind power, biofuel etc.

$G_W = f(Re) = -rRe$
$\Delta G_W / \Delta Re = -r$ where, $r > 0$, it indicates the marginal propensity to use renewable energy.

Greenhouse Gases – Global Warming Function

The more GHGo increases, the more the global warming increases. There is a positive relationship between G_W and GHGo

$G_W = f(GHGo) = g GHGo$

$\Delta G_W / \Delta GHGo = g$ where, g is the marginal propensity of GHGo

Global Warming -Thermal Energy caused by friction Function

The more the thermal energy caused by friction increases, the more the global warming increases. There is a positive relationship between GW and Tec

$G_W = f(Tec) = e\, TEc$

$\Delta GW / \Delta TEc = e$ where, e = the marginal propensity of thermal energy

AntiGreenhouse Gases – Global Warming Function

The more AntiGHGo increases, the more the global warming decreases. There is a negative relationship between G_W and AntiGHGo

$G_W = f(AntiGHGo) = y\, AntiGHGo$

$\Delta G_W / \Delta AntiGHGo = y$ where, y is the marginal propensity of AntiGHGo

Who Are Responsible for Global Warming

Human beings create global warming. Nature have no power to create global warming. We, the human beings, are responsible for increasing global warming. We are decreasing the number of trees per square kilometer for making furniture, building living places and manufacturing various products from trees. As a result, we get low amount of oxygen from air but we produce carbon dioxide more than necessary in air. The lower capital than necessary begets the lower production. The lower production than necessity are responsible for inflation. Like this way we begets global warming by getting lower amount of O_2 and releasing more CO_2 in air. How many trees should need for a square kilometer land according to the density of population is unknown to us. I think it is time to calculate the number of trees in a square kilometer by research. It is not necessary to travel another planet like The Mars. It is necessary to find out how many trees we need a square kilometer land to get enough oxygen. Lack of oxygen we produce Carbon dioxide more than necessary.

How to Reduce the Global Warming

To reduce global warming we have to increase the marginal propensity to plant trees and use renewable energy so that CO_2 can not increase. If we use more fossil fuels we will increase more CO_2. So we have to minimize CO_2. There is positive relationship between CO_2 and global warming. If CO_2 increases, global warming will increase. We know that a matured leafy tree produces 260 pounds O_2 in a year and this will do enough for two men according to *Environment Canada, Canada's national environmental agency. They said,"* "On average, one tree produces nearly 260 pounds of oxygen each year. Two mature trees can provide enough oxygen for a family of four."
According to NC State University, "a tree can absorb as much as 48 pounds of CO_2 per year."

If we combine two concepts, we get, 48 pounds CO_2 = 260 pounds O_2
1 pound CO_2 = (260 / 48) pounds O_2 = 5.42 pounds O_2
*Therefore , **1 kiloton CO_2 = 5.42 kiloton O_2***
That is, If we want to remove 1 kt CO_2, we need 5.42 kt O_2.
In 2018 the number of world population is 7.594×10^9 according to The World bank Data Group.
O_2 needs in 2018 for the whole population
= $7.594 \times 10^9 \times 130$ pounds
= 987.22×10^9 pounds
= (987.22×10^9) / 2204.6 ton
= 447800054.43 ton O_2
= (447800054.43 / 1000) kt O_2
= 447800.054 kt O_2
Suppose, for all animals O_2 need in 2019 ,
 4 times x human beings required O_2
= 4 x 447800.054 kt O_2
= 1791200.22 kt O_2
= (179200.22 / 5.42) kt CO_2
= 330479.74 kt CO_2
But in 2014 we, the inhabitants of the earth, produced 36138285 kt CO_2 according to the World Bank Data Group. This amount is increasing day by day. In 2019 the earth need 330479.74 kt CO_2 but we produced 36138285 kt CO_2 in 2014 by cutting down trees, using fossil fuels (i.e. coals, gases, oils) . Extra amount we produced 5 years ago (36138285 − 330479.74) = 35807805.26 kt CO_2 which was **108.35 times more.** The gigantic problem is this amount CO_2.
On the other hand, the world has only 39958245.9 square kilometer forest land. How many trees are there in a square kilometer forest land ? We don't know. But we know we

are minimizing forest land by cutting trees for making furniture, using industrial purposes etc.

Suppose, T matured leafy trees are in one square kilometer. The number of trees in the world in 2016 is $39958245.9 \times T$ trees.

They produced $3995845.9\ T\ (260/2204.6)$ ton
$= 3995845.9\ T \times 0.12$ ton
$= 479501.508T$ ton O_2
$= 479501.508T\ /\ 1000$ kt O_2
$= 479.502T$ kt O_2

The Green World

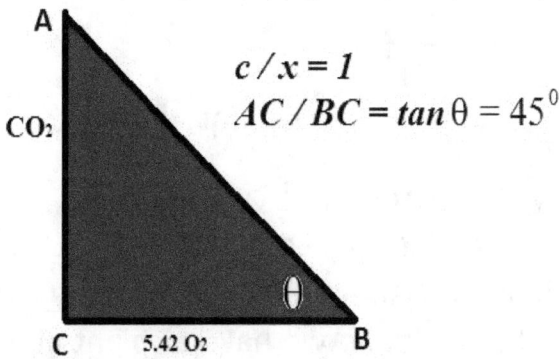

Figure : The Green World

In green world level, $CO_2\ /5.42\ O_2 = 1$
In the figure, According to the right angle triangle ABC,
$\tan\theta = AC/BC = CO2/O2 = 1 = 45$ degree
In the green world level, everywhere we will find trees and trees. The world will seem to be a big jungle. The inhabitants of the world will overcome natural disasters and live happy naturally. The proportion of the marginal propensity of using fossil fuels and the tree plantation will

same, there have no extinction of any animal. There will establish ecological balance.

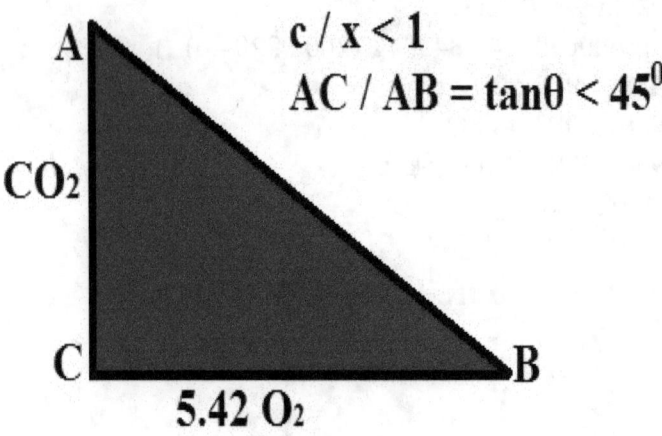

Figure: The Healthy Dreamy World

When, the world reach $CO_2 / 5.42\ O_2 < 1$, then the world will be called Dreamy Healthy World. I think every man needs at least 226 trees to exist in the world. So we have to plant at least 226 trees per capita. By planting trees we can save many men and women and wild lives and maintain ecological balance.

Turning the Present World into the Green World

The present world will be unsuitable for living by 2050. Many animals will extinct by this time. So it is high time we, the people of the world, increased the marginal propensity to produce oxygen and decreased the marginal propensity of carbon emissions so that we can turn the present world into the green world. According to my model when we reach $c = x$, we will make the existing world the green earth.

For increasing the number trees we have to take the following steps.

The marginal propensity to plant trees should be greater than the marginal propensity to cut down trees.

that is, $p > d$ Where, $p, d > 0$

p = the marginal propensity to plant trees,

d = the marginal propensity to cut down trees

if $p > d$ then the world people can increase the number of trees. that means $x = p - d$ where, $x > 0$

If $p < d$, then the world people can decrease the number of trees for their extinction.

That means $x = p - d$ where $x < 0$ which we the world people have created. For this we are facing global warming. To save the world against global warming we should increase the value of x.

The United Nations, World Bank and climate related organizations should encourage the world people to plant trees. The botany experts should research for knowing how much O_2 (oxygen) produce per tree. We should plant the tree which produces the largest amount of oxygen .

To save the world against the global warming we should decrease the value of w . To minimize the amount of carbon dioxide we have to use more renewable energy than fossil fuels.If the marginal propensity to use fossil fuels is less than the marginal propensity to use renewable energy , we will decrease the value of w. Besides ,We should be aware of using the things which produce the greenhouse gases.

The Botany experts should find out how many trees need for one square kilometer forest land and find out the tree that produce more oxygen than normal tree.

We always remember that space travelling is less important than tree plantation. The earth is the only place for animals living because $CO_2 O_2$ cycle exists only this planet and the central point of the universe is here . I have discovered the central point of the universe by my Universal Model. Finally I would like to say " First save the earth against global warming then research another planets.

Analysis of the collected data

Year	Population (Billion)	ΔP	Forest Area (Sq.km)	ΔF	CO_2 Emission (Kiloton)	ΔCO_2	GW (°C)
1999	6.035	-	40628689.7	-	24059187	-	
2000	6.115	0.080	40556022.3	-72667.4	24689911	630724	0.40°
2001	6.194	0.079	40510303.3	-45719	25276631	586720	
2002	6.274	0.08	40464584.1	-45719.2	25646998	370367	
2003	6.353	0.079	40418865.2	-45718.9	27047792	1400794	
2004	6.432	0.079	40373146	-45719.2	28393581	1345789	
2005	6.513	0.081	40327427	-45719	29490014	1096433	
2006	6.594	0.081	40293287.6	-34139.4	30568112	1078098	
2007	6.675	0.081	40259147.7	-34139.9	31180501	612389	
2008	6.758	0.083	40225008.7	-34139	32181592	1001091	
2009	6.841	0.083	40190869.1	-34139.6	31891899	-2829693	
2010	6.923	0.082	40156729.7	-34139.4	33472376	1580477	
2011	7.004	0.081	40123639.2	-33090.5	34847501	1375125	
2012	7.087	0.083	40090560.5	-33078.7	35470891	623390	
2013	7.171	0.084	40057482	-33078.5	35837591	366700	
2014	7.256	0.085	40024403.3	-33078.7	36138285	300694	0.75°
		ΣΔP = 1.221		ΣΔF = -604286.4		ΣΔCO2 = 9539098	

Data source :
World Bank Data Group (Population, Forest Area and $CO2$ Emissions)   and NASA(Global warming)

ΔP = current year – previous year,
ΔF = Current year – previous year ,
ΔCO_2 = Current year – previous year

The average value of ΔP from 2000 to 2014
$= \Sigma \Delta P / n = 1.221 / 15 = 0.814$
The average value of ΔF from 2000 to 2014 $= \Sigma \Delta F / n = -604286.4 / 15 = -40285.76$ sq.km. The average value of ΔCO_2 from 2000 to 2014 $= \Sigma \Delta CO_2 / n$
$= 9539098/15 = 635939.87$ kt

Comment: there is positive relationship between Population and Carbon dioxide but negative relationship between population and forest area. So lack of sufficient oxygen the world temperature is increasing gradually.

The velocity of CO_2 emissions from 2000 to 2014 (VCO_2)
$= (36138285 - 24689911) / 15$
$= 763224.93$ kt
The velocity of forest area from 2000 to 2014(VF)
$= (40024403.3 - 40556022.3) / 15$
$= -531619$ square land
Suppose, the number of trees per square km $= T$
According to Canada Environment Agency,
1 matured tree produces $O_2 = 260$ pounds.
According to them,
A tree produces O2 $= 260 / 2204.6 = 0.12$ ton
We know that 1000 ton = 1 kiloton
T trees produce O_2 per square kilometer $= 0.12T$ ton
The velocity of O_2 from 2000 to 2014 (VO_2)
$=$ VF x $0.12T$ ton $= -531619$ x 0.12 T ton
$= -63794.28$ T ton
$= -63794.28$ $T / 1000 = -63.79T$ kt
Every year we lose O_2 63.79 T kt (approximately)
So we, the inhabitants of the earth, should produce 2 times of 63.79 T kt O_2 per year for saving the world.

The velocity of the global warming from 2000 to 2014
(VGw) = (0.75 – 0.40) / 15 °C = 0.023 °C
The velocity of Population growth = (7.256 x 10^9 - 6.115 x 10^9) / 15 = 1.141 x 10^9 / 1 = 76066666.67
From the above discussion , It can be said that in nature there are negative relationship between global warming and forest areas which produce O_2 for maintaining ecological balance. **So only through increasing forest area global warming can be minimized.**

O_2 inhaled from air in 2014
= (Total forest area x 0.12 T) / (7.256 x 10^9) ton per person
= (40024403.3 X 0.12 T) / (7.256 x 10^9) ton per person
= 4802928.396 T / 7256000000 ton per person
= 0.00066 T ton / person

CO2 exhaled in air in 2014 year
= 36138285 / (7.256 x 10^9) kt/ person
= (3.6138285 x 10^7) / (7.256 x 10^9)
= 3.6138285 / 7.256 X 10^2
= 3.6138285/ 725.6
= 0.0049805 kt/ person
= 4.9805 ton/ person

According to NC State University , a tree can absorb as much as 48 pounds of CO_2 per year.
So , 48 pounds = 48 /2204.6 ton = 0.022 ton (approximately)
The number of trees is needed for absorbing CO_2
= 4.9805 / 0.022 trees per person
= 226 trees (Approximately)

A human being should plant 226 trees (approximately) for saving the world against climate change and global warming.

According to World bank Data Group, in 2000
Carbon emissions 24689911 kt,
Methane(CH_4) Emissions 6480650 kt (equivalent CO_2),
Nitrous oxide emissions 2920510 kt (equivalent CO_2)
According to NASA, Global Warming 0.40° in 2000
So, $Gw = CO_2 + CH_4 + N_2O + GHGo$
0.40° Gw = (24689911 + 6480650 + 2920510) kt + GHGo
Or, 0.40° Gw = 34091071 kt CO2 + GHGo
Or, 1° Gw = 85227677.5 kt CO2 + (GHGo / 0.40°)
Or, 1° Gw = 85227677.5 kt CO2   [(GHGo / 0.40°) ≈ 0]
So, 1° Gw = 85227677.5 kt CO2 (approximately)

It is high time we planted at least 226 tree plants wherever we like for saving our next generation against global warming and climate change.

Result of the Theory

In micro model,

$w = c\ (x)^{-1}$ where, $c > 0$, $x > 0$ and if $w > 1$ then the global warming exists

$\theta = w\ (90/100)$ degree adjacent angle

Gw = Global warming = $\theta / 66.02328 T^{-1}$ °C

1 pound CO_2 = 5.42 pounds O_2 [approximately]
1 kiloton CO_2 = 5.42 kiloton O_2 [approximately]
If we want to remove 1 kt CO_2,
we need 5.42 kt O_2. [approximately]

Suppose, T matured leafy trees are in one square kilometer one square kilometer forest land produces $0.12T$ kt O_2

one degree Celsius Global warming = $66.02328T^{-1}$ degree adjacent angle

one °C global warming is equal to ($48184380 + a$) kiloton CO_2

Macro model,

$GW = hP$

$= KCO_2 + g\ GHGo + eTEc - sO_2 - r\ RE - y\ AntiGHGo$

Global Warming depends on population behavior.

To remove global warming every person needs to plant 226 trees for saving the world and our future generation. Otherwise, you may become the richest person in the world but you will not be able to save your life against global warming.

I think, by applying this model we, the inhabitants of the world, can minimize 0.30 °C global warming within 5 years and within 20 years we will get the healthy dreamy world.

www.ingramcontent.com/pod-product-compliance
Lightning Source LLC
Chambersburg PA
CBHW070426220526
45466CB00004B/1562